PRAYER:
THE TIMELESS
SECRET
OF HIGH-IMPACT
LEADERS

PRAYER:
THE TIMELESS
SECRET
OF HIGH-IMPACT
LEADERS

DAVE EARLEY

LIVING
INK
BOOKS
Writing Worth Reading

ISBN 978-089957031-0
First printing—June 2008
Cover designed by Meyers Design, Houston, Texas
Interior design and typesetting by Reider Publishing Services,
    West Hollywood, California
Edited and Proofread by Rich Cairnes, Dan Penwell, Sharon Neal,
    and Rick Steele

Printed in the United States of America
14 13 12 11 –V– 7 6 5 4 3

Library of Congress Cataloging-in-Publication Data
Earley, Dave, 1959-
  Prayer : the timeless secret of high impact leaders / Dave Earley.
    p. cm.
  Summary: "All other factors being equal, the common denominator of great
spiritual leaders and dynamic spiritual influencers throughout the ages lies
in their prayer lives. Tracing the lives of high impact Christian leaders
from Abraham to Billy Graham, Dave Earley reveals the central role prayer
played in their effectiveness"--Provided by publisher.
  Includes bibliographical references.
  ISBN 978-0-89957-032-7 (pbk. : alk. paper)
  1. Prayer--Christianity. 2. Leadership--Religious aspects--Christianity.
I. Title.
  BV210.3.E255 2008
  248.3'2--dc22

                              2008016807

Contents

Acknowledgments

THERE ARE many people I need to thank for shaping my life of prayer and for helping make this book a reality.

Thanks to Lee Simmons, Roy Rhoades, Drew Aquino, and Steve Ebert who got me started in a life of prayer.

I am extremely grateful for the giants who led the way in prayer, both those from the Bible, from church history, and those who are writing history today.

I also deeply appreciate my students at Liberty University and Liberty Theological Seminary who challenge me to live what I teach.

I am indebted to my co-laborers and teammates at the Center for Ministry Training: David Wheeler, Neil Grobler, Chip Stallings, David Brinkley, Don Hicks, and Gabriel Turner.

I am very grateful to Dan Penwell and the AMG staff who minister out of a deep passion to equip the church.

Thanks to my bosses, Dr. Ergun Caner, Dr. Elmer Towns, and Dr. Daniel Mitchell for giving me an opportunity to research and teach this information.

I want to especially thank my precious family who believe in me when no one else does.

Introduction

DO YOU hunger to influence people for God?

Would you love to become a more effective leader?

Is it your passion to make a deeply positive spiritual difference in the lives of as many people as possible?

If so, I want to help you get there. Or, I should say, God will help you get there. But you need to follow his plan and use the device he has prescribed as the nonnegotiable tool in every high-impact leader's tool kit—prayer.

"Leadership is influence."

These were the words that rang out from the grizzled man whose voice had lost much of its power. But that did not matter to any of us. We had come to hear him. Many will agree that the speaker, J. Oswald Sanders (1917–1992), was one of the finest Christian leaders and teachers of spiritual leadership in the twentieth century.

Dr. Sanders served as a Christian leader for nearly sixty years and authored more than forty books on the Christian life. He left a promising law practice in his native New Zealand to serve as an instructor and administrator at the Bible College of New Zealand.

He later became general director of the China Inland Mission (now known as OMF International) and was instrumental in beginning many new mission projects throughout East Asia.

When I heard he would be in my area, I rearranged my schedule to hear this veteran leader and teacher share insights on leadership in what was one of the last talks he gave before he departed to heaven. Even though he lacked the physical robustness of his earlier years, Sanders did not disappoint. In his lecture, he made several statements that made so much sense they have been deeply unforgettable.

"Leadership is influence,"[1] he said with piercing passion. He continued, "Since leadership is the ability to move and influence people, the spiritual leader will be alert to discover the most effective way of doing this."[2] Then he reached a crescendo with his main point: "Prayer influences men by influencing God to influence them."[3]

Read that last sentence again slowly. That is the essence of this book. Leadership is influence. One of the most powerful ways to influence others spiritually is through prayer. Therefore, to lead effectively by influencing others for God, Christian leaders must pray. If leaders want to lead well, they must pray well.

Over the past thirty years, I have studied the lives of dozens of God's greatest spiritual leaders from Abraham to Billy Graham. It is my conclusion and conviction that prayer is the timeless, and often overlooked, secret to high-impact spiritual leadership. Certainly courageous acts, fearless faith, spiritual gifts, and anointed abilities help make leaders spiritually influential. I agree that credible integrity, fervent passion, clear purpose, and wise plans are important. It is good to cast your vision, identify your values, and build your team. But the common denominator of great spiritual leaders and dynamic spiritual influencers down through the ages lies in their prayer lives. Prayer is the ageless act of highly effective Christian leaders. Prayer must not be slighted. Prayer must be prioritized and practiced to achieve maximum impact.

Prayer, the Common Denominator

Prayer is certainly not the only act of leadership, but it is the indisputable common denominator of spiritual difference-makers in every generation and in any setting. I doubt that you can find a maximally effective spiritual leader in the Bible or in history who was not a person of prayer. This is the reality today as much as it was two thousand years ago. Listen to the voices of renowned authorities in the realm of spiritual leadership.

Henry Blackaby states, "More than any other single thing leaders do, it is their prayer life that will determine their effectiveness."[4] Peter Wagner (1930–) said, "Great leaders pray!"[5] Charles Swindoll (1934–), best-selling author, megachurch pastor, and former president of Dallas Theological Seminary, writes, "Prayer . . . is absolutely essential in the life of a leader."[6]

Wesley Duewel was the leader of OMS International, a large mission agency. Regarding the importance of prayer in the life of a leader he writes, ". . . as a leader your usefulness is dependent upon your prayer"[7] and "the effectiveness of your ministry depends on your spiritual life."[8]

Nineteenth-century Christian leader Andrew Murray (1828–1917) said that prayer in the life of the leader should be regarded "as the highest part of the work entrusted to us, the root and strength of all other work . . . there is nothing we need to study and practice as the art of praying alright."[9]

J. C. Ryle (1816–1900), another well-known nineteenth-century Christian leader, wrote,

"I have read the lives of many eminent Christians who have been on earth since Bible days. Some of them, I see, were rich, and some poor. Some were learned, some unlearned . . . some were Calvinists, and some were Arminians . . . But one thing, I see, they all had in common. They all had been men of prayer."[10]

E. M. Bounds (1835–1913), who spent the last seventeen years of his life locked away given to studying, writing, and practicing prayer, wrote, "Great praying is the sign of God's great leaders."[11] He also said, "Old Testament history is filled with accounts of praying saints. The leaders of Israel in those early days were noted for their praying habits. Prayer is the one thing which stands out prominently in their lives . . . They were essentially men of prayer."[12]

A study of the truly great spiritual leaders reveals that their gifts, talents, personalities, backgrounds, education, and social status varied. But they all had one common denominator—they were people of prayer. I agree with J. O. Sanders, who concluded, "The eminence of great leaders in the Bible is attributable to the fact that they were great in their praying."[13]

My goal in writing this book is simple: I hope to motivate Christian leaders to pray more fervently, more frequently, more effectively, and more contagiously than ever before. I want to stretch their prayer life.

If you have a greater prayer life, you can have greater kingdom influence for God.

It Works

Since I was sixteen years old and found myself leading a Bible study group of teens at our public high school, I have been aware of the link between prayer and impact. I was newly committed to God and entirely insufficient to make much of a difference in anyone's life, so I had no choice but to pray. The more I prayed the more God worked. My group of two turned into several groups of more than thirty. Soon much of our high school was ablaze for God.

As a discipleship pastor for a university, a church planter, and a church pastor, I have been reminded repeatedly that the effectiveness of my leadership life has flowed out of the strength of my prayer life. When I prayed well, impact increased. When I failed to pray, effectiveness diminished.

I have provided leadership in a country church, on a college campus, and at a suburban megachurch, and in settings as diverse as the streets of New York City, the marketplaces of England, and new church starts around the country. I have trained pastors and church leaders in almost all fifty states, and in many foreign countries. Again and again, I have seen the same thing—all other factors being equal, prayer is the common denominator of effective spiritual leadership. Whether you are leading a small group or a university, prayer makes the difference.

Nine Prayer Disciplines of High-Impact Spiritual Leaders

My mother was a librarian and I have always loved biographies. Over the past thirty years I have worn out nearly a dozen Bibles reading the stories of God's leaders from Noah up through the early church. I have also read several dozen biographies of spiritual leaders since Jesus, wearing out paperback versions of the stories of such giants as John Wesley, Charles Spurgeon, Hudson Taylor, and D. L. Moody.

In my pursuit of the factors that made them so successful, I have identified nine prayer disciplines seen in the lives of those who have most effectively led others for God. Applying these nine often-overlooked prayer lessons will focus, stretch, rekindle, and renew your prayer life. They will also make you a more effective spiritual leader.

Only God can judge the true greatness of a leader. For this work, I tried to study many of the best-known names in the Bible and church history. Of those people chosen, all had a marked spiritual impact. They cover a variety of leadership posts—missions, pastorate, education, and parachurch ministries. They span the theological spectrum of evangelicalism.

The quotes and anecdotes came from leaders of whose prayer lives I could find good evidence and information. Some of the ones listed led extremely large works, while others led smaller ministries. Yet all made a marked spiritual difference.

In this book I use anecdotes, quotes, and examples from the lives of seventy-seven spiritual leaders. Some of my information came from the lives of spiritual giants. I have also used some accounts of lesser-known leaders, including my own life. I'm in no way a giant—far from it. I'm an ordinary person like you with a desire to become a leader better able to make a greater impact for God.[14]

CHAPTER 1

Value the Power of Prayer

If You Want to Maximize Your Impact, Prioritize Your Prayer Life

I have trained pastors, missionaries, church staffs, and small-group leaders all over the United States and in many parts of the world. When we discuss prayer, all will nod their heads and agree that prayer is important. Yet, too often, North American Christian leaders are guilty of doing nearly everything else but pray. One survey said the average pastor prays only seven minutes a day![1] Another said 80 percent of pastors surveyed spend less than fifteen minutes a day in prayer.[2]

The most generous survey said pastors pray all of thirty-seven minutes a day. But it also showed that only 16 percent of Protestant ministers across the country are very satisfied with their personal prayer life. This survey stated that a disheartening 21 percent typically spend fifteen minutes or less per day in prayer.[3]

I'm not sure which survey is most accurate, but they all tell us that most pastors pray too little. No wonder so many pastors are discouraged. No wonder so many will burn out. No wonder so many quit.

Church-growth experts have stated that 85 percent of the churches in America are declining in size. Of the 15 percent that are growing, only 1 percent are growing through conversion.[4] Isn't it entirely possible our *ineffectiveness in ministry* can be traced to our *lack of prayer?*

All other factors being equal, the difference between effective and ineffective spiritual leaders is prayer. As you assemble your personal leadership tool kit, be certain to add the instrument of prayer. As you evaluate your leadership quotient, be careful not to neglect prayer. If you want to maximize your impact, prioritize your prayer life. Effective spiritual leaders value the power of prayer.

Prayer Is the Most Important Task of the Spiritual Leader

There are many important tasks for the leader. Planning, vision casting, team building, communicating, and policy making are important responsibilities for an effective leader. But Christian leadership is *spiritual* work. *Spiritual* work depends upon *spiritual* tools. No spiritual tool is as significant or powerful as prayer. As Andrew Murray reminds us, "In spiritual work everything depends upon prayer."[5]

The importance of prayer in effective spiritual leadership shows up on every level of Christian leadership. For example, a survey of small-group leaders revealed an interesting correlation between time spent in prayer and small-group multiplication. It revealed that leaders who spent ninety minutes or more in daily devotions multiplied their groups *twice as often* as those who spent less than half an hour.[6]

Taking the time to pray makes a difference! Success here will make success in the other areas much easier. Failure here will make success in the other areas nearly impossible.

The responsibilities of spiritual leaders have deep eternal ramifications. The burden for eternal souls is often complex and confusing, immense and exhausting. Henry and Richard Blackaby get to the heart of this matter when they write:

> There will be times when leaders will come to the end of their own resources. In those times they will understand there is nothing more they can do for their people. Giving speeches will not fix the problem. Issuing memos will change nothing. Calling in consultants will be futile. There are simply some things that can only be achieved through prayer (Psalm 50:15).[7]

Prayer Is the Most Influential Activity a Leader Can Undertake

When I look at the massive responsibility of trying to influence people for God, I'm stunned by my own insufficiency. Who am I? When it comes to worldly influence, I'm a "nobody." I can't do it. But I know someone who can—God. He can do more in a tiny fraction of a second than I can accomplish in years. He can do it better, bigger, and more permanently than I can even *imagine.*

So the question becomes, how can I somehow influence God to be more influential in the lives of the people I'm responsible for? The answer, of course, is prayer.

Charles Spurgeon (1834–1892) was an incredibly effective spiritual leader. He served as pastor of one of the few megachurches of his time and founded a pastor's training college. In speaking of the influential nature of prayer, he called it "the slender nerve that moves the muscles of omnipotence."[8]

R. A. Torrey (1856–1928) was an American evangelist, pastor, educator, and writer. He served as head of the Bible Institute of the Chicago Evangelization Society (now Moody Bible Institute); dean of Bible Institute of Los Angeles (now Biola University). He pastored two of the largest and most influential churches of his time—Chicago Avenue Church (now Moody Memorial Church) in Chicago, and Church of the Open Door in Los Angeles. Torrey made an astounding observation when he wrote, "Prayer is the key that unlocks all the storehouses of God's infinite grace and power. All that God is and all that God does is at the disposal of prayer. But we must use the key. Prayer can do anything God can do, and as God can do anything, prayer is omnipotent."[9]

Hudson Taylor (1832–1905) was an English missionary to China. He founded the China Inland Mission, which became miraculously influential for God in China. At his death, the mission included 205 mission stations with more than 800 missionaries and 125,000 Chinese Christians.

How did he do it?

He said he discovered "[i]t is possible to move men through God by prayer alone."[10]

The words of the powerful revivalist Leonard Ravenhill (1907–1994) remind us that *"Prayer is as vast as God* because He is behind it. Prayer is as mighty as God because He has committed Himself to it."[11]

Church historians will recognize the name of John Chrysostom (c. 347–c. 407). He was a church leader who was considered one of the most eloquent, yet powerful, preachers who ever lived. He understood the amazing power available through prayer:

> The potency of prayer hath subdued the strength of fire; it hath bridled the rage of lions, hushed anarchy to rest, extinguished wars, appeased the elements, expelled demons, burst the chains of death, expanded the gates of heaven, assuaged diseases, repelled frauds, rescued cities from destruction, stayed the sun in its course, and arrested the progress of the thunderbolt. Prayer is the all-sufficient panoply, a treasure undiminished, a mine never exhausted, a sky unobscured by clouds, a heaven unruffled by storm. It is the root, the fountain, the mother, of a thousand blessings.[12]

Prayer Saves Time

Everyone is busy, especially leaders. There is always another meeting to attend, another person to see, another event to plan. We never seem to have enough time.

One of the biggest excuses made for not praying enough is that we are too busy. Such a statement reveals a fundamental misunderstanding about the nature and power of prayer. To think we are too busy to pray shows a failure to understand that prayer actually saves time and effort.

Prayer allows God to do more in days, hours, minutes, or even seconds than we could accomplish without him in months, or even years, of work. How often have we taught, encouraged, and counseled people with little or no result? How often have we shared our faith with seemingly little or no breakthrough in the other person's defenses? But, when God moves, he helps people make changes in seconds that we could not get them to make in years. Prayer is a powerful time-saver. Once we understand this principle, we will learn to say, "I'm too busy *not* to pray."

Martin Luther (1483–1546) towers as a giant in church history. The highly active and influential pastor, professor, author, and father of the Protestant Reformation understood the power of prayer to save time and effort. When asked of his plans for the coming week, Luther mentioned that he generally spent two hours a day in prayer, but the coming week was extra busy. Therefore, he said, "Work, work from early till late. In fact I have so much to do that I shall spend the first *three* hours in prayer."[13]

Three hours in prayer on a busy day?

The average pastor may spend three hours in prayer during a leisurely week!

Maybe Martin Luther understood something you and I need to grasp. Time spent praying can be the best time-saving device you have.

I doubt that anyone ever comes to the end of life saying, "I prayed too much." But many come to the end of their lives saying, "I prayed too little."

What would happen if you prayed more than ever before? What could it hurt? Whom might it help?

Prayer Is Omnipresent

Nearly every summer, I have the rich privilege of spending a few days training missionaries to the least-reached people on earth— Hindus, Muslims, and Buddhists. These leaders are some of God's greatest unsung heroes. Often the "retired" missionaries join us.

One evening I was dining with a couple who had given their lives trying to plant churches in Iran. This sweet couple told me with deep humility and joy how they are just now seeing seeds of their labor sprouting into churches all over the region in which they served. I showed my ignorance when I said, "I bet you miss being over there serving and encouraging those saints."

The husband shook his head and explained, "We get to bless Iran every morning and every evening, on our knees, praying in our bedroom. Our ministry to Iran is much larger now than it ever was when we lived in Iran."

Effective leaders understand the unrestricted reach of prayer. As a leader, I'm often frustrated by the fact that I cannot be in two places at once. But God can. As a parent I'm limited in that I cannot be with my sons when they go off to school or work. But God can.

One of the amazing aspects of prayer is that it is unlimited by day and time, location, or distance. Prayer invites God to work in people's lives even when church is not in session or the small group is not meeting. You can't meet with all your members twenty-four hours a day, but God can. You can't go with all your members to their homes or with them to work, but God can. You can't be in two or more places at once, but God can.

It is thrilling to think I can be on my knees in Virginia and at the same moment be ministering to pastors in Africa or encouraging missionaries in Asia. S. D. Gordon understood this well when he said, "Prayer opens a whole planet to man's activities."[14]

Wesley Duewel (1918–) has been a high-impact leader in world missions for nearly seven decades. He understands the geographically unlimited possibilities of prayer. "Through prayer you can accompany any missionary to remote reaches of the earth. Through prayer you can walk through crowded bazaars, minister in steaming jungles, feed millions of starving men, women, and children, hungry for bread for their bodies and for the Bread of Life."[15]

Prayer Is the Determining Factor

The more I study spiritual leadership and see how it works in daily life, the more I'm convinced prayer is the determining factor. The difference between mild stirrings and deep breakthroughs is prayer. The difference between a temporary inclination and a lasting change is often prayer. The difference between mediocrity and greatness is frequently prayer.

The more we pray, the more God works. The more God works, the better everything will ultimately be. We fail to recognize the astounding way our omnipotent God has linked his activity to our prayers.

The prophet Ezekiel showed how the prayers of a single intercessor would have been the determining factor in delivering Israel from the Babylonian captivity:

> I looked for a man among them who would build up the wall and stand before me in the gap on behalf of the land so I would not have to destroy it, but I found none. So I will pour out my wrath on them and consume them with my fiery anger, bringing down on their own heads all they have done, declares the Sovereign LORD. (Ezekiel 22:30, 31)

Read those verses again, slowly. Think about the fact that one single gap-stander could have stopped the Babylonian captivity. But the last four words of verse 30 tell the sad story—*"but I found none."*

Through the years I have found I am not alone in my belief that prayer was the determining factor. This truth is echoed from one end of the theological scale to the other. On one pole of the theological continuum, we have John Wesley (1703–1791), who wrote, "God will do nothing on earth, except in answer to believing prayer." On the other pole we have John Calvin (1509–1564), who in his *Institutes of the Christian Religion* states, "Words fail to explain how necessary prayer is . . . while God never slumbers or sleeps He is inactive, as if forgetting us, when He sees us idle and mute."[16]

Billy Graham (1918–) has observed, "Today the world is being carried on a rushing torrent of history. There is but one power available to redeem the course of events, and that is the power of prayer. . . ."[17]

Others have agreed. Slowly read their words:

When we pray we are working with God to determine the future. Certain things will happen in history if we pray rightly.—Richard Foster[18]

When God finds a person who will place as his priority a life of intimate, personal, dynamic fellowship with Him, He directs His power, guidance, and wisdom into and through that person. God has found a man through whom He can change the world.—LeRoy Eims[19]

You and I can help decide which of these two things—blessing or cursing—happens on earth. We determine whether God's goodness is released toward a specific situation or whether the sower of sin and Satan is permitted to prevail. Prayer is the determining factor . . . If we don't, He won't.—Jack Hayford[20]

God has of His own motion placed Himself under the law of prayer, and has obligated himself to answer the prayers of men. He has ordained prayer as a means whereby He will do things through men as they pray, which He would not otherwise do . . . man has it in his power to by prayer, move God to work in His own way among men, in which way He would not work if prayer was not made.—E. M. Bounds[21]

I don't fully understand it, but I know that the more we pray, the more God works. The more God works, the better things end up being. On many levels prayer *is* the determining factor of spiritual leadership.

Prayer Provides Insight

Solomon faced the impossible task of taking over leadership from a living legend, his father, David. God graciously promised to give Solomon anything he asked for. So with dependent humility he sagely prayed, "Give me wisdom and knowledge, that I may lead this people, for who is able to govern this great people of yours?" (2 Chronicles 1:10).

Solomon's request for wisdom pleased the Lord and was abundantly granted. God loves to answer the prayer of leaders for wisdom (James 1:5).

True prayer not only speaks, but also listens. Prayer connects us with God, and God knows everything. When we listen in prayer, God gives us insight into important matters. Suddenly, we have fresh perspective on a complex situation, or we may gain new understanding of the needs, strengths, struggles, and potentials of those we are privileged to lead. Through prayer we are able to discern the key to unlock the heart of a difficult person, or recognize the right person to hire, or know when to delegate an important responsibility, or recognize whom to recruit as a potential leader.

God Does Nothing in Ministry Apart from Prayer

Ministry is, at its core, spiritual work. Prayer is spiritual work. David Jeremiah (1941–) leads a megachurch in southern California and a Christian college. Regarding the essential role in ministry, he writes,

> I scoured the New Testament some time ago, looking for things God does in ministry that are not prompted by prayer. Do you know what I found?
>
> Nothing.
>
> I don't mean I had trouble finding an item or two: I mean I found nothing. Everything God does in the work of ministry, He does through prayer. Consider:
> - Prayer is the way you defeat the devil (Luke 22:23; James 4:7).
> - Prayer is the way you get the lost saved (Luke 18:13).
> - Prayer is the way you acquire wisdom (James 1:5).
> - Prayer is the way a backslider gets restored (James 5:16–20).
> - Prayer is how saints get strengthened (Jude 20; Matthew 26:41).
> - Prayer is the way to get laborers out to the mission field (Matthew 9:38).
> - Prayer is how we cure the sick (James 5:13–15).
> - Prayer is how we accomplish the impossible (Mark 11:23, 24).
>
> . . . everything God wants to do in your life; He has subjugated to one thing: Prayer.[22]

Billy Graham (1918–) is one of the best-loved spiritual leaders of the last century. He has been called "the nation's pastor." He once said his ministry was built on promotion and prayer. He believes in the untapped power of prayer:

More can be done by prayer than anything else. Prayer is our greatest weapon . . . In this modern age in which we live, we have learned to harness the power of the mighty Niagara and turn its force to our use and our good. We have learned to hold steam captive in boilers and release its tremendous power to turn our machines and pull our trains. We have learned to contain gasoline vapors in a cylinder and explode them at the appointed second to move our automobiles and trucks along our highways. We have even discovered the secret of releasing energy in the atom, which is capable of destroying entire cities and civilizations. But very few of us have learned how to fully develop the power of prayer.[23]

Prayer Is Our Greatest Spiritual Weapon

The apostle Paul was no stranger to spiritual conflict. His record includes shipwreck, hunger, thirst, and severe floggings. Five times he endured the brutal "forty lashes minus one." Three times he was beaten with the Roman rods. Once he even endured a stoning! He wrote many of his letters from prison. In fact, in his letter to the Ephesian church, he explained the real source of the absurd level of adversity and opposition: "For our struggle is not against flesh and blood, but against the rulers, against the authorities, against the powers of this dark world and against the spiritual forces of evil in the heavenly realms" (Ephesians 6:12).

He went on to detail the believer's protection through the armor of God. Interestingly, he closes his discussion of spiritual warfare with an appeal to prayer:

And pray in the Spirit on all occasions with all kinds of prayers and requests. With this in mind, be alert and always keep on praying for all the saints. Pray also for me, that whenever I open my mouth, words may be given me so that I will fearlessly make known the mystery of the gospel, for which I am an ambassador in chains. Pray that I may declare it fearlessly, as I should. (Ephesians 6:18, 19)

No one has offered spiritual leadership for long without running into serious spiritual conflict. Effective leaders win the lost and reproduce themselves by equipping leaders to take ground from Satan, and he does not like it. Effective spiritual leaders recognize the necessity and power of prayer in spiritual warfare.

We are hearing more and more accounts of church members and churches bound by demonic oppression. As the occult has become part of mainstream culture in America (notice the nature of the movies shown in theatres around Halloween), the strongholds of the enemy have increased and multiplied.

We are seeing an increased level of satanic attack on spiritual leaders in North America. Again and again, I have listened as broken pastors and weeping spouses recount eerily similar tales of recurring nightmares, strange illnesses, and unexplainable opposition. More and more leaders, whose theological backgrounds don't usually recognize such things, tell me of wrestling with dark forces in difficult settings.

Spiritual leaders must pray to keep from being defeated by Satan's persistent attacks on them and on their churches. When it comes to spiritual warfare, to fail to pray is to fail altogether. Satan will not let you simply plunder his kingdom. He will not just allow you to grow and multiply, evangelize, and equip. He will fight you every inch of the way.

We must not only pray to keep from losing ground, but also pray in order to take ground. On our own, we are not more powerful than the Enemy, but we are when we pray. We can fight him successfully from our knees. We can march forward on our knees. Only one weapon will hold him off and push him back. It is the weapon of prayer. This is why we must pray without ceasing.

As a missionary statesman, S. D. Gordon (1859–1936) traveled to many of Satan's strongholds and gained a deep understanding of the vital power of prayer in spiritual warfare. He wrote, "In its simplest meaning, prayer has to do with conflict. Rightly understood it is the deciding factor in a spirit [sic] conflict . . . Prayer is man giving God a footing on the contested territory of this earth. . . ."[24]

Chuck Smith (1927–) understands the necessity and potential power of prayer for waging spiritual warfare. He has said, "Through prayer you can advance with the battering ram and demolish the strongholds the enemy has on those individual lives—freeing them from the power that holds them captive."[25]

Dick Eastman (1946–) is the president of Every Home for Christ. This international ministry has a full-time staff of more than 1,200, plus more than 14,000 volunteer associates; has systematically distributed more than 2.4 billion gospel messages, house to house, in 196 nations of the world, resulting in more than 52.7 million decision cards being mailed to EHC's many offices overseas and the establishing of more than 111,000 village churches. He understands leadership, prayer, and spiritual warfare, and elevates the importance of prayer in spiritual conflict. He writes, "Prayer is not so much another weapon on our list of weaponry as it is the actual battle."[26]

We need more men and women of God who will train in spiritual warfare and become mighty in prayer. A missionary leader, burdened by the gaping desperate needs in our world, cried, "We seem to have ten thousand prayer amateurs for one true prayer warrior."[27] Will you become a prayer warrior?

Pray or Quit!

"Then Jesus told his disciples a parable to show them that they should always pray and not give up" (Luke 18:1).

Pray or quit. That's the choice Jesus knew his disciples would face. He knew that the relentless rigors of high-octane ministry would wear or burn them out if they did not develop a prayer life.

The pace would be too demanding, the opposition too brutal, people problems too frequent, and the need too overwhelming.

If anyone has seen the reality of "pray or quit," it is Joe McKeever (1940–), who ministers to pastors and churches trying to rebound from the horrific devastation of Hurricane Katrina in New Orleans. With great wisdom he writes:

> If anyone on planet Earth needs to pray faithfully and fervently, it's the pastor. For one thing, this job requires more of you than there is and more time than you have. The person accepting the Lord's call into the ministry is agreeing to live in a world of unfinished tasks. You are literally being sentenced to live beyond yourself.
>
> It is by its very nature impossible to live this life and do this work in your own strength. You will develop a strong prayer life or you will not survive. It's as simple as that.[28]

We are told an increasing number of pastors leave the ministry because of burnout or moral failure.[29] A stunningly high number of pastors and their spouses feel unqualified, discouraged, and disillusioned in their role in ministry.[30] Nearly 25 percent of pastors have been terminated at some time in their vocation. Kevin Miller, an editor for *Christianity Today*, concludes that "Pastoring is increasingly like coaching pro football: being under [intense] pressure is part of the territory."[31]

What can be done so those of us in various Christian leadership positions won't give in or give up in the face of mounting pressures? Why not start where Jesus suggested—always praying so we don't lose heart?

Longtime missionary leader Wesley Duewel points out, "Your task as a Christian leader is too big for you. Its immensity and awesomeness must drive you to prayer. Your vocation is too large for you and your calling too sacred for you. But God is available for your ministry if you are willing to pay the price in prayer."[32]

You can make a difference. You can hang in there.

Are you willing to pay the price in prayer?

Why Not?

My goal in writing this book is very simple. I want to challenge you as a leader to develop a strong and effective prayer life. I seek to instruct you, and to inspire you to pray more often, more effectively, and more contagiously than ever before. Why not make the investment?

Why not start now?

Why not take some time praying about your prayer life?

Why not watch less TV this week and spend more time praying?

Why not surf the Internet less this week and spend more time praying?

Why not begin each day by talking to God?

Why not talk with God on your way to work this week?

Why not talk with God as you fall asleep tonight?

Why not make a few special appointments to pray this week?

Why not?

APPLICATION WORKSHEET

What are two or three key thoughts you want to remember from this chapter?

1.

2.

3.

Check the boxes of the specific applications you plan to work on.

This week I propose to deepen and strengthen my prayer life by:

- ☐ 1. Watching less TV and/or spending less time on the Internet, and spending more time praying.
- ☐ 2. Starting each day by talking to God.
- ☐ 3. Talking to God on my way to work this week.
- ☐ 4. Talking with God as I fall asleep each night.
- ☐ 5. Making a special appointment for extra prayer one day this week. That day will be _____.
- ☐ 6. Lengthening my daily prayer time to _____ minutes.
- ☐ 7. Other: _____
  _____
  _____
  _____
  _____

CHAPTER 2

Make Time to Pray

Who IS the ideal model for all Christian leaders to follow?

Is it a legendary football coach?

Is it the successful CEO of a large corporation?

Is it the well-known pastor of a large church?

While we can certainly learn from coaches, CEOs, and pastors, shouldn't Jesus be first on the list of those we seek to emulate? Isn't he our example? Are we not to walk in his footsteps?

Yes, I have heard the argument that "we can't model ourselves after Jesus because he was the Son of God, and, well, we aren't." True. But too often we so emphasize his deity that we forget his humanity. Jesus was 100 percent God, but he was *also 100 percent human*. He was not only the Son of God, but he called himself the Son of *Man*. He voluntarily submitted himself to the same frustrations, limitations, and temptations we face. As a human he grew hungry, tired, and frustrated.

Jesus knew and lived the life of human leadership. We need to adopt Jesus Christ as the foundation on which everything we learn about leadership is built and the template on which everything we learn about leadership is hung.

Jesus Christ: Man of Prayer

Making Jesus our primary pattern for learning leadership means we need to do what he did. One of the chief leadership skills Jesus practiced was prayer. Jesus Christ was an amazing man of prayer.

S. D. Gordon summarized well the prayer life of the leader Jesus when he wrote, "The *man* Christ Jesus *prayed*; prayed *much*; *needed* to pray; *loved* to pray."[1] He added, "Jesus prayed. He loved to pray . . . He prayed so much and so often that it became a part of His life. It became to Him like breathing—involuntary."[2]

E. M. Bounds concurs: "Prayer filled the life of our Lord while on earth . . . Nothing is more conspicuous in the life of our Lord than prayer."[3]

Yes, I have heard the argument that we cannot pray like he did because he was the Son of God. But here is the point: If Jesus Christ, the Son of God, needed to pray, *how much more* do you and I?

In the Gospels, there are fifteen accounts of Jesus praying. Eleven are found in Luke's gospel. Why? The answer is that of the writers of the four Gospels, Luke focused most on the *human* aspect of Jesus. Luke wanted us to see that as a *human* leader, Jesus lived a life of prayer. Jesus was fully God *and* fully man. If Jesus, the human, needed time to pray, how much more do you and I?

Prayer—First Things First

Mark's gospel was tailored to the active lifestyle of the Romans. In chapter 1, Mark records a sample twenty-four-hour time period in the life of Jesus. It's a day that nearly rivals one of Jack Bauer's days spent saving the world from terrorists. In the span of twenty-four hours, Jesus gave an amazing teaching at the synagogue (vv. 21, 22); cast a violent, belligerent demon out of a man (vv. 23–28); and healed Simon Peter's mother who in gratitude, got up and fixed a lunch for Jesus and his disciples (vv. 29–31). He then spent the rest of the day and late into the night healing sick people and casting demons out of the terrorized (vv. 32–34). Whew!

I cannot imagine a more draining day. If he were like most of us, after such a draining day of ministry, the next morning would have been spent sleeping in and chilling out. But Jesus lived and led at a different level. He had a deep capacity for ministry because he practiced a few holy habits that yielded powerful results.

Was Jesus sleeping in the next day? No. Read verse 35 carefully: "Very early in the morning, while it was still dark, Jesus got up, left the house and went off to a solitary place, where he prayed."

Prayer was the first of Jesus' daily activities and appointments, the number one item on his calendar each day. If nothing else would get done that day, prayer would get done.

Like Jesus, I also like to have my main prayer time first thing in the morning. I have learned that if I don't pray first thing in the morning, I often don't get to it. I have learned that if I start my day in prayer, the rest of the day always goes better.

Many other high-impact spiritual leaders down through the centuries have been practitioners of early morning prayers. For example, King David wrote, "In the morning, O LORD, you hear my voice; in the morning I lay my requests before you and wait in expectation" (Psalm 5:3).

Martin Luther was a busy guy. He pastored a church, taught in a seminary, wrote extensively, translated the Bible into German, and in his spare time, sparked the Protestant Reformation! He also was an advocate of praying first thing in his day. "If I fail to spend two hours in prayer *each morning*, the devil gets the victory through the day."[4]

The biographers of Hudson Taylor, the intensely busy founder of the China Inland Mission, described the priority Taylor gave to prayer and Bible study. Taylor found it necessary to meet God very early in the day. When I say "very early," I mean *very early*. His biographers write, "From two to four a.m. was the time he usually gave to prayer, the time when he could be most sure of being undisturbed to wait upon God."[5] At the age of seventy Taylor is quoted as telling one of his children, "I have just finished reading the Bible through, today, for the fortieth time in forty years."[6]

One of the biographies that most impacted my life is the life story of Dawson Trotman (1906–1956), founder of the Navigators. He was a very ordinary man with an extraordinary passion for God and prayer who launched a worldwide organization that especially left a deep spiritual impact on the U.S. Navy in World War II. As a young man he often met God early in the morning in the hills of Southern California to pray.

Once he covenanted to pray two hours early every morning before work for forty straight days. Near the end of the forty days, he and a prayer partner prayed over a map of the world. Amazingly, before he died at the young age of fifty (while saving someone from drowning), Trotman saw the fruit of his labor spanning the globe in answer to those early prayers. His biographer writes, "Dawson held on to his consuming purpose to become a man of God, a man of prayer . . . in looking back later, he had little doubt that his disciplined practice of prayer during the first five years of his Christian life laid a foundation for all of his subsequent ministry."[7]

John Wesley (1703–1791), one of the voices of the First Great Awakening and the father of Methodism, started each morning with one to two hours of prayer.

Passionate pastor Robert Murray McCheyne (1813–1843) said, "I feel it is far better to *begin with God*—to see His face first, to get my soul near Him before it is near another."[8]

I have the privilege of teaching at a seminary with nearly one hundred students from South Korea. As you probably know, the church in Korea has grown explosively the last few decades. One of the many things I love about these students is their willingness to pray. Many of them gather every morning at 5:30 in our prayer chapel for an hour of prayer.

While rare in North America, such early-morning prayer meetings are common in South Korea. For example, Peter Wagner tells of attending the early-morning prayer gatherings at Myong-Song Presbyterian Church in Seoul. The church had daily prayer meetings at 4:00 a.m., 5:00 a.m., and 6:00 a.m. with a total attendance of twelve thousand![9] No wonder the number of Christians in South Korea has risen so dramatically the last several decades. Imagine—on August 15, 1988, one million Korean Christians gathered at an outdoor stadium to pray.

One Korean pastor whose church numbers hundreds of thousands of members writes, "I'm not able to do all that I have been called to do without spending the minimum of one hour in prayer every morning."[10]

Too Busy Not to Pray

Jesus bit off life in big chunks and often ministered at an intense pace. The demands on his time and energy were immense. His inner strength was repeatedly tapped by slow-to-grasp-the-truth disciples, vast crowds, desperately needy sick and demonized people, and fierce opposition. Everything he did went against the grain of the Jewish leaders and their extremely legalistic religion. How did he survive it, let alone thrive through it and rise triumphantly above it all?

Jesus viewed prayer as the secret source of spiritual strength and the reservoir of real refreshment. Even when he was very busy, he was never too busy to pray.

Bill Hybels (1952–) wrote a book with the insightful title *Too Busy Not to Pray*. In it he makes this admission: "Prayer has not always been my strong suit. For many years, even as a senior pastor of a large church, I knew more about prayer than I ever *practiced* in my life. I had a racehorse temperament, and the tugs of self-sufficiency and self-reliance are very real to me."[11]

Hybels mentions the frequent sense of feeling "overwhelmed, overrun, beaten down, pushed around, and defeated" that resulted from his weak prayer life. He proceeds to tell how he then obeyed the promptings of the Lord to study and practice prayer. He then describes the refreshing and quantitative difference in his relationship with God that flows from "carrying on substantial soul-searching conversations every morning for a good chunk of time."[12]

The leader of a huge church in South Korea, writing on the importance of leaders taking the time to pray, has written, "One of the greatest lies of Satan is that we don't have enough time to pray. However, all of us have enough time to sleep, eat, and breathe. As soon as we realize that prayer is as important as sleeping, eating, and breathing, we will be amazed at how much time we have to pray.[13]

George Müller (1805–1898) was one of the most amazing spiritual leaders the world has ever seen. He was a gifted philanthropist and evangelist. He circulated 111 million tracts and pamphlets, 1.4 million New Testaments, and 275,000 Bibles in different languages, with nearly as many smaller portions of Scripture. He supported 189 missionaries. After he turned seventy, he preached the gospel in forty-two nations to approximately three million people. During his life, he cared for more than ten thousand orphans, provided education for 123,000 students, and received $7,500,000 of unsolicited funds from human sources by faith and prayer alone.

As a young minister, when he was starting his orphanages, Müller went through a very busy season. In fact, he often found himself too busy to pray as he ought. His biographer wrote, "After learning the lesson of being busy in the work of the Lord, too busy in fact to pray, he told his brethren that four hours of work after an hour of prayer would accomplish more than five hours without prayer. This rule henceforth he faithfully kept."[14]

Charles Spurgeon, the incredibly successful and busy English pastor, agreed. When preaching on the subject of prayer he observed,

Sometimes we think we are too busy to pray. That also is a great mistake, for praying is a saving of time . . . God can multiply our ability to make use of time. If we give the Lord his due, we shall have enough for all necessary purposes. In this matter seek first the kingdom of God and his righteousness, and all these things shall be added to you. Your other engagements will run smoothly if you do not forget your engagement with God.[15]

Establish a Daily Prayer Time

Jesus prayed first thing in the morning (Mark 1:35). He also prayed late at night (Mark 6:46; Luke 6:12, 13; Matthew 26:36–44). Peter and John observed at least an afternoon time for prayer, as did Cornelius (Acts 3:1; 10:3). Peter is also shown to be praying at noon (Acts 10:9). Paul and Silas prayed and sang hymns at midnight (Acts 16:16).

John Bunyan (1628–1688) was an English pastor who was jailed in the mid- and late seventeenth century for preaching the gospel. His book, *The Pilgrim's Progress*, is the second most popular book on earth, next to the Bible. He was an advocate of early-morning prayer and said, "He who runs from God in the morning will scarcely find him the rest of the day."[16]

Martin Luther said, "It is a good thing to let prayer be the first business of the morning and the last at night."[17]

When Jerry Falwell (1933–2007) was a college student, he learned the immense value of having a daily prayer time. He went to the dean of students and asked for a key to the third floor of the administration building. There he prayed from 1:30 to 5:00 every weekday afternoon, crying out to God to bless his ministry as a fifth-grade Sunday school teacher. It paid off. The class grew from two boys to fifty-seven.[18]

One of the most important questions we can ask a person who aspires to authentic spiritual leadership is "*When* do you pray? *When* is your time with God?"

I don't believe *the* time for prayer is always as important as at least having *a* time of prayer each day. When I first began to walk with the Lord as a high school student, my daily time with God was at night, after dark. I added prayer to my evening run and loved it. During my first year of college the only time my dorm was quiet was over the lunch hour, so that became my time to spend alone with God in Bible study and prayer. My sophomore year, my time with God was after dinner. My junior year, it was in the afternoon. Now I have two primary times: One is first thing in the morning. After I read my Bible, I pray using my journal. Then I get ready for work. On the drive to my office I have my second main prayer time as I pray some more, usually about other issues.

Most of us need to set a daily prayer time or times if we hope to build a dynamic prayer life. We may choose morning, afternoon, or evening, but we need to at least choose a time, or several times, for prayer.

Pray Several Times a Day

A study of the life of highly effective spiritual leaders reveals that many observed *a series of set prayer times each day.* The great leader King David mentions that for at least one season of his life he cried out to God in prayer three times during the day—morning, noon, and evening (Psalm 55:17).

Jewish-born Daniel was an alien in the foreign, pagan land of Babylon. He was an outstanding leader. When trouble hit, it was good that cabinet member Daniel had established a regular ongoing practice of praying three times a day (Daniel 6:10).

Possibly because they were motivated by the example of David and Daniel, the pattern of prayer three times daily was adopted by the Jews and was regularly practiced up through the time of the early church. Regarding the Jewish pattern of prayer, Epiphanius speaks of "rising up in the morning and in the middle of the day and in the evening, three times a day, when they say their prayers in the synagogue."[19]

The early church continued the practice. For example, church father Tertullian (c. 160–c. 225) said explicitly that we must always pray and adds these significant words: "As regards the time, there should be no lax observation of certain hours—I mean of those common hours which have long marked the divisions of the day, the third, the sixth, and the ninth, and which we may observe in Scripture to be more solemn than the rest."[20]

At the time he wrote those words, the day started at 6 a.m. Therefore, "the third, the sixth, and the ninth" hours represented 9 a.m., noon, and 3 p.m.

Many of the early church leaders observed more than three daily prayer times. For example, Hippolytus (d. 235), in the beginning of the third century, spoke of praying six times a day:

> If you are home, pray at the third hour and bless God. But if you are somewhere else then, pray to God in your heart . . . Pray likewise at the sixth hour . . . Let a great prayer and a great blessing be offered also at the ninth hour . . . Pray as well before your body rests on its bed. But toward midnight rise up, wash your hands and pray . . . And at the cockcrow rise up and pray once more.[21]

At the age of twenty-five, Adoniram Judson (1788–1850) was the first Protestant missionary sent from North America to minister in Burma (now known as Myanmar). Although he waited six years for his first convert, he later planted churches and translated the Bible into Burmese. Sometime after his death a government survey recorded 210,000 Christians, one out of every fifty-eight Burmese!

Judson's advice to rising spiritual leaders is very challenging: Pray seven times a day!

Endeavor seven times a day to withdraw from business and
company and lift up thy soul to God . . . Begin the day
by rising after midnight and devoting some time amid
the silence and darkness of the night to this sacred work. Let
the hour of opening dawn find thee at the same work. Let the
hours of nine, twelve, three, six, and nine at night witness
the same. Be resolute in thy cause. Make all practical sacrifices to maintain it. Consider that thy time is short and that
business and company must not be allowed to rob thee of
thy God.[22]

Determine an Amount of Time to Pray

Effective spiritual leaders not only establish a time for prayer but
also usually set *an amount of time*. Most set aside an hour, many
set aside even longer.

> I imagine that the pattern of spending an hour in prayer goes
> back to the Garden of Gethsemane, where Jesus confronted the
> sleeping apostle Peter: "Then he returned to his disciples and
> found them sleeping. 'Could you men not keep watch with me
> for one hour?' he asked Peter. 'Watch and pray so that you will
> not fall into temptation. The spirit is willing, but the body is
> weak.'" (Matthew 26:40, 41)

Many have taken this question personally and have made the
effort to give God an hour of prayer each day. Think about it. An
hour a day would add up to 365 hours a year, or the equivalent of
more than forty-five eight-hour days. That's a month and a half a
year spent in prayer! Just think what God could do through you,
for you, and in you and those you pray for *if* you prayed an hour
every day!

Institute a Regular Place for Prayer

Almost as important as the time of prayer is the *place* of prayer. Mark 1:35 speaks of Jesus selecting a secluded, silent place. Undisturbed, he was able to focus on the business at hand, meeting his Father in prayer. In the Sermon on the Mount, Jesus mentioned going into your room and closing the door when you pray (Matthew 6:6).

The best example of a leader having a special place for prayer is Moses. The people Moses led were mostly spiritual infants. He had to teach them everything, including how to relate to God. One of his best teaching tools was his practice at a place he called the *Tent of Meeting*.

> Now Moses used to take a tent and pitch it outside the camp some distance away, calling it the "tent of meeting." Anyone inquiring of the LORD would go to the tent of meeting outside the camp. And whenever Moses went out to the tent, all the people rose and stood at the entrances to their tents, watching Moses until he entered the tent. As Moses went into the tent, the pillar of cloud would come down and stay at the entrance, while the LORD spoke with Moses. Whenever the people saw the pillar of cloud standing at the entrance to the tent, they all stood and worshiped, each at the entrance to his tent. The LORD would speak to Moses face to face, as a man speaks with his friend. (Exodus 33:7–11)

As you read through Exodus, when you get to chapter 33, the dust is still settling. The Exodus account slows down, pulls back, and tells us some things about life among the nomadic Israelites. I especially love the little picture we are given regarding "the tent of meeting."

That tent was a place made sacred because divine dialogue occurred there. When Moses went inside, distractions were minimized. It also made the meeting time special. Bill Hybels writes, "Once you identify such a place and begin to use it regularly, a kind of aura surrounds it. Your prayer room, if it is a laundry room in the basement, becomes to you what the Garden of Gethsemane became to Jesus—a holy place, the place of meeting with God."[23]

In his classic book *With Christ in the School of Prayer*, Andrew Murray (1828–1917) addressed the value of having a meeting time and place if the spiritual leader is to truly learn to pray: "He wants each one to choose for himself that fixed spot where He can daily meet him. That inner chamber, that solitary place, is Jesus' schoolroom. That spot may change from day to day; but that secret place there must be . . . there alone, but there most surely, Jesus comes to teach us to pray."[24]

I have found it to be very helpful to have a set, solitary place for my daily prayer time as I attempt to build a dynamic prayer life. Through the years the place has changed. When I was in high school, it was in the woods or along a running path. In college, my prayer place was an empty dorm room. For several years, I prayed while prayer-walking my neighborhood. For another season, I prayed at my desk in the office of my church each morning.

Most recently my main prayer places are my chair in the family room before anyone else is up and my car on the way to work. To me these are sweet and sacred places because I have met God there in prayer. Fears have been expressed, burdens lifted, answers secured, and direction given.

The Operating Room

During my first semester at college, my prayer place was an operating room. That was one of my best prayer places of all. Let me explain.

My college was so young it did not even have dorms. I found myself living with a few dozen other young men crammed into a forsaken hospital in the ghetto of a small city four hundred miles from home. Four of us shared a room and eight of us a bathroom. There were no closets and little privacy. However, the best thing I remember about that hospital/makeshift dorm was the operating room.

The bad news was I had classes at 7:00 a.m. daily. The good news was that I was done with classes and back at the hospital by noon. Someone had wisely designated the upstairs operating room as the dorm prayer room, so no one lived in it. The only furniture was a cold, gray, metal desk and a stiff metal chair—which was fine by me. It also had a large window overlooking the street below, aptly named Grace Street.

I decided I needed to have an hour alone with God, so I locked myself in the prayer room at noon, every day Monday through Friday. For the first half hour I let God speak to me through his Word. I usually read a Psalm and wrote in a small notebook what I thought God was saying to me through that Psalm. The second half hour I spoke with God. I used a plan called the "ACTS" plan of prayer (Adoration, Confession, Thanksgiving, Supplication—we'll discuss this in detail in a later chapter), and recorded my requests in a notebook.

After the first few days of getting used to having a daily, sit-down appointment with God, I found myself longing for that time in the operating room each day. I would scramble back from class and dash up the stairs to the prayer room in order to not be late for my twelve o'clock appointment with God. Every day God was faithful to meet me at exactly noon and operate on my heart. Each day the Chief Surgeon of Grace Street would cut a bit deeper with his Word. Each day he would speak healing and hope to my heart in prayer.

Oh, I wish I had the words to convey how sweet, how amazing, how real it was to meet with God an hour each day! I would love to begin to explain how much it changed and enriched my life. If only I could list all the answers to prayer I'm seeing today that were requests made back there in that operating room.

But I can't. I don't have the skill, or the time, or the space. But I think you might have an inkling of how amazing it was for me to sit across the desk from my Creator, my Redeemer, my Father, and my Best Friend every day.

Jews view Jerusalem as holy ground. Muslims think of Mecca as sacred. Cubs fans view Wrigley Field as hallowed ground, but to me nothing compares with that operating room. I met God there. What more can I say?

We moved to real dorms after several months and I found another place for prayer. But nothing will ever take the place of that operating room. In fact, a few years later I had the opportunity to go back to that hospital for a few minutes. Anxiously I climbed the stairs to the operating room. Cautiously I opened the door. Breathlessly I peered inside and gasped. I was not prepared for what happened next.

The table and chair sat there in the center of the room, just as we had left them. But they were not all that was still there. A hundred memories of a hundred hours spent seeking God's face were there. A tidal wave of emotions swept over me and tears filled my eyes. This was where I had gone to new depths and greater heights in loving God. This was where I had been schooled in the prayer life.

Another important question we can ask a person who aspires to authentic spiritual leadership is, "*Where* do you pray?" "*Where* is your solitary meeting place(s) with God?"

Take the Time

I don't know how much you pray now, but I want to encourage you to pray more. If my words are not enough, let these statements from two spiritual masters provoke you to be intentional about taking time for prayer:

There can be no communion with a holy God, no fellowship between heaven and earth, no power for the salvation of souls, *unless much time is set apart for it.*—Andrew Murray[25]

Much time spent in prayer is the secret of all successful praying. Prayer that is felt as a mighty force is the mediate or immediate product of much time spent in prayer. Our short prayers owe their point and efficiency to the long ones that have preceded them.—E. M. Bounds[26]

How to Make Time to Pray

1. Remind yourself of the value and power of prayer.
2. Determine a time or times when you will pray each day.
3. Decide on the amount of time you plan to spend praying each day.
4. Choose a place or places to have your prayer times.
5. Do it!

APPLICATION WORKSHEET

What are two or three key thoughts you want to remember from this chapter?

1.

2.

3.

When is (or will be) your daily *time* or *times* for prayer?

What is (or will be) your *amount* of time for prayer?

Where is (or will be) your *place* or *places for prayer?*

CHAPTER 3

Pray for Those You Serve

Effective Spiritual Leaders
Pray for Their People

Effective spiritual leaders are passionate toward God *and* compassionate toward people. God gives us a burden, a holy concern, for those we are called to lead. We may not always accept their behavior, but we have a genuine love for them.

One of the purest and most powerful ways for a leader to express and exercise such love is in intercessory prayer. "Love on its knees" is the definition and description Dick Eastman gives to intercessory prayer.[1] Such prayer seeks the best for others before the throne of God and brings their needs to the One who has the answers.

A study of the lives of high-impact spiritual leaders reveals that they take time to pray for their people. Consider Moses. His primary ministry as he led the Hebrews through the wilderness can be summarized in six simple words:

"So Moses prayed for the people." (Numbers 21:7)

Moses was an unusually effective spiritual leader, in part because he prayed, or *interceded*, for his people. The term *intercede* means "to go between." Used for prayer it describes the act of going to God and pleading on behalf of another.[2]

Prayer as a general term describes talking to God. Intercession is more specific. It describes coming to God *on behalf of another*. Therefore, while all intercession is prayer, not all prayer is intercession.[3]

Intercession was a major part of the leadership ministry of Moses. Again and again in the books of Exodus and Numbers, we hear Moses effectively crying out to God on behalf of his followers (Exodus 17:4; Numbers 11:2; 14:13–19).

Too many Christian leaders pray too little and too many Christian leaders pray too little for others. This must change. Intercessory prayer is a primary tool used by effective spiritual leaders.

The great leader and prophet Samuel felt it was sinful to fail to pray for his people. He said to his people, "As for me, far be it from me that I should sin against the LORD by failing to pray for you" (1 Samuel 12:23).

Missionary leader Wesley Duewel writes, "You have no greater ministry or no leadership more influential than intercession."[4]

It was E. M. Bounds who said, "Talking to men for God is a great thing. But talking to God for men is greater still."[5]

S. D. Gordon said, "True prayer never stops in petition for one's self. It reaches out for others. Intercession is the climax of prayer."[6]

Jesus is the Great Intercessor. His entire ministry is identifying with us, standing in our stead, and going to God the Father on our behalf. As a leader, he prayed for his followers. In speaking of the Twelve, he said, "I pray for them" (John 17:9). In speaking of his then-future followers, like us, he said, "I pray also for those who will believe in me through their [the disciples'] message" (John 17:20). Even now in his exalted home in heaven, Jesus is the One "who is even at the right hand of God, who also makes intercession for us" (Romans 8:34 NKJV), he is the one who "always lives to make intercession" for us (Hebrews 7:25 NKJV).

The apostle Paul was a major league difference-maker. Note that his letters are washed in mention of his intercessory prayers for his followers:

> God, whom I serve with my whole heart in preaching the gospel of his Son, is my witness how constantly I remember you in my prayers at all times. (Romans 1:9, 10)

> I have not stopped giving thanks for you, remembering you in my prayers. (Ephesians 1:16)

> In all my prayers for all of you, I always pray with joy. (Philippians 1:4)

> For this reason, since the day we heard about you, we have not stopped praying for you. (Colossians 1:9)

> We always thank God for all of you, mentioning you in our prayers. We continually remember before our God and Father your work produced by faith, your labor prompted by love, and your endurance inspired by hope in our Lord Jesus Christ. (1 Thessalonians 1:2, 3)

> With this in mind, we constantly pray for you. (2 Thessalonians 1:11)

> I thank God, whom I serve, as my forefathers did, with a clear conscience, as night and day I constantly remember you in my prayers. (2 Timothy 1:3)

If we want to lead like Moses, Paul, or Jesus, we need to pray like Moses, Paul, and Jesus. Like them we must pray for our followers.

Effective Spiritual Leaders Elevate
Their Followers over Themselves

Moses knew that one of the baseline attitudes of an effective leader is that the people come ahead of the leader. In Exodus 32:9–10, in a stunning announcement, God offered to destroy the people of Israel and start over, making Moses into a great nation. Wow! All Moses' whiny headaches would be gone, *and* he could become the father of a nation—heady stuff for anyone to consider.

But Moses did not even give it a moment's thought. Instead, he immediately set out asking God to spare the people.

But if that seems like a supreme act of selflessness, Moses takes it a step further. One of the most stunning, revealing, and challenging verses in the Bible on the subject of great leadership is found at the end of Exodus 32. The people had sinned yet again. Moses responded by interceding with God to spare the rebellious Hebrews under his care: "So Moses went back to the LORD and said, 'Oh, what a great sin these people have committed! They have made themselves gods of gold. But now, please forgive their sin— but if not, then blot me out of the book you have written'" (v. 31).

I'm amazed at the sacrificial selflessness of Moses: *"Forgive their sin—but if not, then blot me out!"* He was willing to lose his own reservation in paradise if it would keep the Hebrews from being destroyed. Moses was a great leader because he was a great servant.

Think about it. Moses was modeling the leadership training of Jesus and doing it 1,450 years before Jesus gave the teaching! No wonder his intercession was so effective. He prayed out of the model of Jesus:

> Jesus called them together and said, "You know that those who are regarded as rulers of the Gentiles lord it over them, and their high officials exercise authority over them. Not so with you. Instead, whoever wants to become great among you must be your servant, and whoever wants to be first must be slave of all.

For even the Son of Man did not come to be served, but to serve, and to give his life as a ransom for many." (Mark 10:42–45)

Great leaders are willing to sacrifice for their followers. Consider the heart of the apostle Paul, who cried, "I could wish that I myself were cursed and cut off from Christ for the sake of my brothers, those of my own race, the people of Israel" (Romans 9:3–4).

Dick Eastman is the president of the large missions agency Every Home for Christ. He also is a prayer warrior and catalyst. He writes, "An intercessor must bid farewell to self and welcome the burdens of humanity."[7] Elsewhere he states, "As intercessors who bear our crosses of sacrifice, we too stand between hurting humanity and a loving Father, carrying their concerns to God."[8]

True Intercession Makes a Huge Difference

The Hebrews, under Moses' watch, were a rebellious lot whose propensity to wander angered the Lord. In fact, on more than one occasion, he was so angry with them that he planned to destroy them. Yet he never did, even though he had good reason.

What affected his decision?

The determining factor was the intercessory prayers of their leader, Moses:

> "I have seen these people," the LORD said to Moses, "and they are a stiff-necked people. Now leave me alone so that my anger may burn against them and that I may destroy them. Then I will make you into a great nation."
>
> But Moses sought the favor of the LORD his God. "O LORD," he said, "why should your anger burn against your people, whom you brought out of Egypt with great power and a mighty hand?" . . . Then the LORD relented and did not bring on his people the disaster he had threatened. (Exodus 32:9–11, 14)

Again and again, the people Moses led complained to God.
Again and again, Moses prayed for his people.
Again and again, God responded to Moses' prayers.

Intercession Brought Revival to a College Campus

History records many times when the intercessory prayers of students shook their campuses for God. For example, on a cold winter day in February 1970, students made their way to the regular chapel service on the campus of Asbury College in Wilmore, Kentucky. For months several student leadership groups had been rising a half hour earlier each day to pray for their campus. Other student groups were also praying diligently for spiritual awakening.

That morning their prayers were answered.

The chapel service, normally fifty minutes in length, ended up lasting more than a week! Day after day students came to the microphone and confessed sins or gave testimony. At the altar and around the auditorium, students gathered in clusters to pray.

After the first day, the revival spread across the street to the seminary. Then it flowed through the community to several local churches. The local and national media picked up the story. People came from several states to get in on what God was doing. Teams of Asbury students visited churches with the message of revival. Several other colleges heard reports of the happenings at Asbury and experienced God's moving on their campuses.[9]

Intercession Made a Difference on My College Campus

I must admit I'm very partial to the power of the intercessory prayers of Moses. Let me explain.

When I was a young man I was given the big responsibility of serving as director of discipleship/campus pastor for three thousand Christian college students. Frankly, I was woefully under-equipped, understaffed, underfunded, and underprepared, and thoroughly overwhelmed. I was also a new husband and a full-time seminary student. Over Christmas break, I found myself worn out and frustrated with several other areas of my life. As a result, I experienced my first real crisis of faith.

So I began a three-day fast, reading through the prayers of Moses and the words of the Psalms. My two biggest questions for God were "Does any of our ministering really matter?" and "Does prayer truly make any difference?"

One passage regarding the prayers of Moses answered both my questions, restored my faith, and changed my life. It was as though the rest of my Bible were printed in black and white, but one verse jumped out like it was written in neon lights: "So he said he would destroy them—had not Moses, his chosen one, stood in the breach before him to keep his wrath from destroying them" (Psalm 106:23).

Had not Moses—those three words in the middle of Psalm 106:23 spoke to my soul. Destruction would have come—*had not Moses*. A nation would have been wiped off the face of the earth—*had not Moses*. History would have been terribly altered—*had not Moses*. Thousands would have died—*had not Moses*.

Think about it. The prayers of one leader spared an entire nation from going into extinction. The intercession of a single spiritual leader changed history for his people. The prayers of one made a big difference for many.

A few days after I read Psalm 106:23 a guest speaker was to come to our campus for a series of special meetings. I shared that verse with the student leaders and challenged them to fervently pray for the students in their dorms.

They did.

Their prayers culminated in a spontaneous, voluntary prayer meeting that lasted all night prior to the speaker's coming. Needless to say, their prayers made a difference for their people, and we experienced a serious, glorious visitation from God through that guest speaker.

God listens when we pray for others. The more we pray, the more God works. God's greatest works are often in response to our greatest prayers. Intercessory prayer is the determining factor, especially for leaders.

Effective Intercession Is Costly

Nehemiah was another great leader with a great prayer life. This seemingly ordinary man led an untrained and fearful group of despairing and desolate former slaves to accomplish a nearly impossible engineering feat in record time against constant and severe opposition. Then he helped lead them to experience a major revival.

In 586 BC, Babylon's king, Nebuchadnezzar, invaded Jerusalem and sacked the city. When Jerusalem fell, the wall was broken down and the city, including the temple and the royal palace, were set on fire. All the survivors, except for the poorest of the poor, were taken into captivity in Babylon.

Forty-eight years later, in 538 BC, the Persian king, Cyrus, destroyed the Babylonian Empire. In that same year he issued a decree permitting the Jews to return to their native land. As a result, Zerubbabel led nearly fifty thousand Jews back to their homeland to settle.

Some eighty years after this, in 458 BC, another return took place during the reign of Artaxerxes I, king of Persia. A scribe named Ezra led this return. This time more than 5,700 people returned to the Promised Land. They began to rebuild the temple.

Yet, the city still lay in ruin and reproach because the protective wall that surrounded it was still broken down. In the ancient world, a city without walls was a vulnerable target for thieving marauders and military invaders. The situation was desperate and when Nehemiah heard about it, he began to pray. "When I heard these things, I sat down and wept. For some days I mourned and fasted and prayed before the God of heaven" (Nehemiah 1:4).

Notice his admission, "When I heard these things, I sat down and wept." The plight of Jerusalem so consumed Nehemiah's mind and heart that he could do nothing other than weep and pray. He shared deeply in the heartache of God for his people in Jerusalem through a ministry of tears.

Spiritual leadership takes on great power and authority when leaders so tightly link their heart with God's that it beats in rhythm with his and they feel his burdens.

Often, tears will be the result.

"Give me souls or I die!"

John Hyde (1865–1912) served as a missionary in India. Difficulties with hearing hindered his learning the language, and his early work was not noteworthy. His deficiencies drove him to desperate, tear-stained prayer. Soon he was spending whole nights in prayer. The nationals called him "the man who never sleeps" because of his long seasons of prayer. He earned the name of "Praying Hyde."

One year John dared to pray what was at that time and place considered an impossible request. He asked that one soul would be saved every day during the coming year in India. Impossible, yet not to the man who sows in tears. That year John prayed more than 400 people into God's kingdom.

The next year he boldly doubled his goal to two souls a day. He prayed and wept and wept and prayed for souls. Eight hundred conversions were recorded that year. Eventually John's ferocious intercessions opened the door for a great evangelistic awakening to sweep down through the entire territory.

One of his biographers spoke of the holy power generated in Hyde's prayer closet. He said that to pray with John Hyde was "to hear the sighing and the groaning, and to see the tears coursing down his dear face, to see his frame weakened by foodless days and sleepless nights, shaken by sobs as he pleads, 'O God give me souls or I die.'"[10]

"Try tears."

Bob Pierce (1914–1978), the founder of World Vision, a huge Christian relief and development organization that works to tackle poverty in more than 100 countries, once wrote on the flyleaf of his Bible, "Let my heart be broken with the things that break the heart of God."[11] God's leaders pray out of hearts crushed by the people and situations that cause God's heart to break.

God told the prophet Joel he wanted his spiritual servants to intercede for their people with tears (Joel 2:17). He gave the same message through Isaiah (Isaiah 22:12). When they refused to do so, God saw their selfishness as "sin that will not be atoned for" (Isaiah 22:14). Likewise, the prophet Samuel took his role in praying for God's people very seriously when he wrote, "As for me, far be it from me that I should sin against the LORD by failing to pray for you" (1 Samuel 12:23).

Wesley Duewel adds, "We must so identify with those we lead, both by love and by commitment, that we carry them on our hearts every day of our leadership . . . we must touch His throne constantly for our people. We sin against the Lord if we fail to do so."[12]

Think of the spiritual leader Jesus, whose heart for hurting people was summed up in two words—"Jesus *wept*" (John 11:35). Consider how he became a man of sorrows and acquainted with grief (Isaiah 53:3). See him lament, "O Jerusalem, Jerusalem . . . how often I have longed to gather your children together, as a hen gathers her chicks under her wings, but you were not willing!" (Luke 13:34). Notice the tears tracing down his cheeks when he contemplated the pain of the people:

> When he looked out over the crowds, his heart broke. So confused and aimless they were, like sheep with no shepherd. (Matthew 9:36 The Message)

> As he approached Jerusalem and saw the city, he wept over it. (Luke 19:41)

During the days of Jesus' life on earth, he offered up prayers and
petitions with loud cries and tears to the one who could save
him from death, and he was heard because of his reverent submission. (Hebrews 5:7)

The lonely trail of tears is a path high-impact leaders travel.
David wept over insults to God's name (Psalm 69:9, 10), Isaiah
wept over the plight of his enemies (Isaiah 6:9, 11), and Josiah
wept for his people (2 Kings 22:19). A crowd gathered as a result
of Ezra's tears (Ezra 10:1, 2).

Jeremiah has been labeled "the weeping prophet." Hear the
deep burden in his words as he writes, "Since my people are
crushed, I am crushed; I mourn, and horror grips me" (Jeremiah
8:21) and "Oh, that my head were a spring of water and my eyes a
fountain of tears! I would weep day and night for the slain of my
people" (Jeremiah 9:1, emphasis added).

Out of anguished love he warned his people, "If you do not
listen, I will weep in secret because of your pride; my eyes will
weep bitterly, overflowing *with tears*, because the LORD's flock will
be taken captive" (Jeremiah 13:17, emphasis added).

Jeremiah wrote another book of the Bible that, because of its
tear-stained content, became known as Lamentations. In it he
records God's grief over the sinfulness of his people and the
destruction of Jerusalem. One of its astounding features is that
the weeping of God results in tears streaming down Jeremiah's
cheeks:

This is why I weep and my eyes overflow with tears. (Lamentations 1:16)

My eyes fail from weeping, I am in torment within, my heart is
poured out on the ground because my people are destroyed,
because children and infants faint in the streets of the city.
(Lamentations 2:11)

Streams of tears flow from my eyes because my people are destroyed. My eyes will flow unceasingly, without relief, until the LORD looks down from heaven and sees. (Lamentations 3:48–50)

Of course, the apostle Paul's ministry is splattered with tears. He summarized his ministry in Ephesus by reminding the elders that he "served the Lord with great humility *and with tears*" and "that for three years I never stopped warning each of you night and day *with tears*" (Acts 20:19, 31, emphasis added). He told the Corinthians "I wrote you out of great distress and anguish of heart and *with many tears*" (2 Corinthians 2:4). The thought of his people, the Jews, not coming to Christ caused him to write, "I have great sorrow and unceasing anguish in my heart. For I could wish that I myself were cursed and cut off from Christ for the sake of my brothers, those of my own race, the people of Israel" (Romans 9:2–4).

William Booth (1829–1912) was an unconventional, controversial zealot for Jesus. He lived the life of a spiritual soldier as the founder of the Salvation Army and preached to the least of the least. Two of his protégés set out to found a new work, only to meet with failure and opposition. Frustrated and tired, they appealed to Booth for permission to close the rescue mission.

General Booth sent back a telegram with only two words on it:

TRY TEARS.

They followed his instruction, and they witnessed a mighty revival.[13]

Influential Intercession Persists until It Receives

Abraham was a flawed but highly influential spiritual leader. He was the spiritual father of the faithful and the biological father of the Jews. One of the strengths in his leadership was that he was mighty in intercession.

God and two angels cloaked themselves in human form and visited Abraham and Sarah to tell them Sarah would bear a child within a year.

After dinner, the three guests got up to leave and the Lord confided in Abraham that they were about to investigate the extreme wickedness of Sodom. Realizing that judgment was about to come, Abraham valiantly positioned himself between the Lord and Sodom and seriously interceded on behalf of the people of that city:

> The men turned away and went toward Sodom, but Abraham remained standing before the LORD. Then Abraham approached him and said: "Will you sweep away the righteous with the wicked? What if there are fifty righteous people in the city? Will you really sweep it away and not spare the place for the sake of the fifty righteous people in it? Far be it from you to do such a thing—to kill the righteous with the wicked, treating the righteous and the wicked alike. Far be it from you! Will not the Judge of all the earth do right?" (Genesis 18:22–25)

There is much to learn from this prayer. Did you notice that Abraham gave God a definite challenge to respond to: "Will you really sweep it away and not spare the place for the sake of the fifty righteous people in it?" (v. 24). Notice how he appealed to the Lord's righteous and just character: "Far be it from you to do such a thing—to kill the righteous with the wicked, treating the righteous and the wicked alike. Far be it from you! Will not the Judge of all the earth do right?" (v. 25).

God listened to the appeals and it profoundly affected him for the sake of the fifty righteous: "The LORD said, 'If I find fifty righteous people in the city of Sodom, I will spare the whole place for their sake'" (v. 26).

Wow! One man's prayers had potentially saved the entire city.

Yet, Abraham was not through. He was not blind and he was no naive fool. He knew the wicked nature of Sodom. He cared enough for the people of Sodom that he had to be sure of their deliverance, so he continued his intercession: "Then Abraham spoke up again: 'Now that I have been so bold as to speak to the LORD, though I am nothing but dust and ashes, what if the number of the righteous is five less than fifty? Will you destroy the whole city because of five people?'" (vv. 27, 28).

God must have smiled when Abraham had the boldness to ask him to spare Sodom again, this time for the sake of forty-five righteous people. "If I find forty-five there," he said, "I will not destroy it" (v. 28).

I probably would have stopped there, content to leave well enough alone. But not Abraham—he was relentlessly aggressive in his prayers. Four more times he sought God on behalf of Sodom. Each time he appealed for greater grace and mercy:

> Once again he spoke to him, "What if only forty are found there?"
>
> He said, "For the sake of forty, I will not do it."
>
> Then he said, "May the LORD not be angry, but let me speak. What if only thirty can be found there?"
>
> He answered, "I will not do it if I find thirty there."
>
> Abraham said, "Now that I have been so bold as to speak to the LORD, what if only twenty can be found there?"
>
> He said, "For the sake of twenty, I will not destroy it."
>
> Then he said, "May the LORD not be angry, but let me speak just once more. What if only ten can be found there?"
>
> He answered, "For the sake of ten, I will not destroy it." (Genesis 18:29–32)

Amazing! One man's persistently insistent prayers secured the safety of an entire city—*if* the city had a representation of a mere ten righteous souls. It took faith to keep coming back to God and asking for more. It took serious concern for those people. It also took holy stubbornness . . . and it worked. God agreed to Abraham's request.

Unfortunately, Abraham had been overly optimistic in his view of Sodom. He must have assumed that surely his nephew Lot would have been able to convert a few others to join him on behalf of God and righteousness. But sadly, as you know, Lot had failed to convert even his own wife. There were not even a handful of righteous people in Sodom. So it was destroyed.

But don't miss the bigger issue. Abraham's intercession had potentially spared Sodom from destruction. Persistent petition makes a difference.

Spirit-Prompted Intercession Wins Lost Loved Ones

Hudson Taylor stands as one of the great missionaries as he pioneered methods that opened China to the gospel. Yet as a teenager he was restless and rebellious. He became the anxious prayer concern of his sister and mother, among others, which led to a story that has become a legend in missions circles.

According to Taylor, in June 1849, when he was seventeen, his mother locked herself in a room fifty miles from home. She was visiting her sister at the time, and she felt moved not only to pray that Taylor would become a Christian but to stay in the room until she was sure her prayers had been answered. That same afternoon, Taylor later recalled, he picked up a gospel tract about the finished work of Christ and accepted "this Savior and this salvation."[14]

Resilient, Triumphant Intercession Converts the Lost

Persistent, faith-based intercession produces results. No one symbolizes this better than George Müller. Once while preaching, Müller testified that forty years prior, in 1844, five individuals were laid upon his heart, and he began to intercede for them to come to Christ.

Müller told how eighteen months passed before one of them was converted.

He prayed on for five years more and another was converted. He continued to pray.

At the end of twelve and a half years, the third was converted.

Müller stated that he had continued to pray for the other two, without missing a single day, but they were not yet converted. He had been praying for these two men daily for forty years, but he was encouraged that the answer would come.[15] In fact, Müller said, "They are not converted yet, but they will be."[16]

Twelve years later, at his death, after interceding for them daily for *fifty-two years*, they still were not converted.

But one came to Christ at Müller's funeral and the other shortly thereafter![17]

Resilient, persistent intercession makes a difference.

How to Intercede More Effectively

Suggestions for Better Intercession

1. Pray for others as you wish others would pray for you.
2. Focus your intercessory prayers more on the spiritual issues of eternal significance than the material, physical, temporal needs of the other person.
3. Use scriptural prayers as appropriate. Below are two prayers Paul prayed for his followers:

For this reason, since the day we heard about you, we have not stopped praying for you and asking God to fill you with the knowledge of his will through all spiritual wisdom and understanding. And we pray this in order that you may live a life worthy of the Lord and may please him in every way: bearing fruit in every good work, growing in the knowledge of God, being strengthened with all power according to his glorious might so that you may have great endurance and patience, and joyfully giving thanks to the Father, who has qualified you to share in the inheritance of the saints in the kingdom of light. (Colossians 1:9–12)

And this is my prayer: that your love may abound more and more in knowledge and depth of insight, so that you may be able to discern what is best and may be pure and blameless until the day of Christ, filled with the fruit of righteousness that comes through Jesus Christ—to the glory and praise of God. (Philippians 1:9–11)

A Guide for Praying for Prodigal Loved Ones

One of the greatest stories ever told is the narrative Jesus gave of the prodigal son. It is the tale of a young man who asked for his inheritance prematurely, then ran off and wasted it in wild living. Finally he came to his senses and went home to his father's house. I love the statement Jesus made revealing the awesome love of the father. "But while he was still a long way off, his father saw him and was filled with compassion for him; he ran to his son, threw his arms around him and kissed him" (Luke 15:20).

Prodigals *do* come home in response to prayer. Maybe you have loved ones who have wandered far from "home." Luke 15 gives a good guide for praying for them:

Lord, *please:*
Bring them to a place of famine and need (v. 14).
Create within them holy hunger and "homesickness" (vv. 16, 17).
Cause them to come to their senses (v. 17).
Draw them home (v. 18).
Give them the gift of repentance (vv. 18–21).
Give us welcoming grace (v. 20).

A Guide for Praying for the Lost and the Backslidden

Sometimes I find it helpful to have an outline to guide me as I pray for others. Below is a suggested outline for praying for those who need Christ:

1. Lord, pour out your Spirit upon (name of person).
2. Convict him/her of his/her sin, lack of righteousness, and deserved judgment (John 16:8).
3. Reveal to him/her who you are and what Christ has done for him/her.
4. Open the eyes of his/her understanding (Ephesians 1:18) and remove his/her spiritual blindness (2 Corinthians 4:4).
5. Draw him/her to yourself in a powerful fashion (John 6:44).
6. Bind Satan from him/her. Keep Satan from stealing your Word from his/her heart (Matthew 12:19).
7. May your grace and mercy surround him/her.
8. Help me to be willing and anxious to be the means by which you save and deliver him/her. Lord, show me how to lead him/her to Christ.
9. Send people across his/her path to bring him/her a witness of Christ.[18]

A Guide for Praying for Your Church

Pray that we would:

- truly love and serve one another (John 13:14).
- be protected from the evil one (John 17:15).
- be sanctified and freed through the truth (John 8:32; 17:16).
- be united (John 17:21–23).
- be, and make, disciples (Matthew 28:19, 20).
- be devoted to the Word, prayer, fellowship, worship, ministry, and evangelism (Acts 2:42–47).

APPLICATION WORKSHEET

What are two or three key thoughts you want to remember from this chapter?

1.

2.

3.

Who do you believe God is prompting you to pray for?

What prayers do you believe you should be praying for them?

CHAPTER 4

Train Others to Pray for You

IN THE EARLY years of my ministry as a spiritual leader, and to my own loss, I overlooked the importance of soliciting prayers from my people. Yet, one day that radically changed. Let me explain.

I woke up one morning in pain. Sharp, stinging pain. I got out of bed and looked down at my arm. Every painful area was marked with an angry red welt. My legs and back were worse, with burning red welts everywhere.

I went to my doctor, who was stunned. "Twenty-two!" he exclaimed, shaking his head. "Twenty-two boils."

"I have only had one boil in my life," I said. "How could I now have twenty-two all at the same time?"

He proceeded to quiz me on everywhere I had been recently, everything I had done, and everything I had eaten. "Uh, uh," he sighed, shaking his head. (I don't like it when doctors shake their heads.)

"I have never seen anything like it . . . so many boils coming so fast," he muttered. "I have never read anything like it . . . except in the book of Job." The light of insight flashed in his eyes. "This is a long shot but it is worth asking. What are you preaching about on Sunday?" (My doctor is a believer.)

"Spiritual warfare," I said. "I'm preaching on the devil and demons."

"Bingo!" he said. "This can only be spiritual warfare."

The coming of the boils and the visit to the doctor happened on a Tuesday. I went home from the doctor's and told Cathy what he had said. She called some of our prayer warriors and asked them to pray for a miracle.

Friday morning I was back at the doctor's. "Gone," he muttered, shaking his head. "All gone. Never seen anything like it. Boils don't come and go that quickly. Your people must have done some strong praying on your behalf." Within two days all the boils were all gone.[1] I was beginning to learn the power of a leader soliciting prayer from his followers.

When we started our church I was ignorant of the Enemy's schemes, and the Enemy took advantage of that. Every Saturday was miserable at my house, especially if we had a big crowd expected on Sunday morning. The kids would be healthy all week but wake up vomiting on Saturday night, or they would be good all week and be rotten on Saturday night, or my wife and I would get along great all week and get in an argument over some stupid little thing on Saturday night. And then, at about midnight, right after we had fallen asleep, the phone would ring. It would either be a wrong number or a drunk.

After a few years of this I began to see a pattern. (I'm a little slow.) So after the boils incident, I swallowed my pride and that Sunday night I explained to my people what was going on and asked them to pray for me, especially on Saturday nights. The next Saturday night was heaven in my home. The kids were happy and healthy. Cathy and I got along great. The phone did not ring. I slept like a baby. That Sunday I preached better than ever.

"Pray for me."

The apostle Paul was one of the most influential leaders in history. He was one of the first missionaries, planted many churches, and wrote thirteen books in our New Testament. He also knew the rigors of spiritual leadership and experienced severe levels of opposition that seem incredible to most of us. On one occasion he summarized some of the adversity he faced as a spiritual leader, compared with his critics:

> I have worked much harder, been in prison more frequently, been flogged more severely, and been exposed to death again and again. Five times I received from the Jews the forty lashes minus one. Three times I was beaten with rods, once I was stoned, three times I was shipwrecked, I spent a night and a day in the open sea, I have been constantly on the move. I have been in danger from rivers, in danger from bandits, in danger from my own countrymen, in danger from Gentiles; in danger in the city, in danger in the country, in danger at sea; and in danger from false brothers. I have labored and toiled and have often gone without sleep; I have known hunger and thirst and have often gone without food; I have been cold and naked. Besides everything else, I face daily the pressure of my concern for all the churches. (2 Corinthians 11:23–28)

How could he endure such intense levels of opposition in the ministry? What was his secret? While he never solicited money from his followers, six times in his letters (and presumably many more times in person) Paul asked the people to pray for him:

- Brothers, pray for us. (1 Thessalonians 5:25)
- Finally, brothers, pray for us that the message of the Lord may spread rapidly and be honored, just as it was with you. (2 Thessalonians 3:1)
- I urge you, brothers, by our Lord Jesus Christ and by the love of the Spirit, to join me in my struggle by praying to God for me. (Romans 15:30)
- Pray also for me, that whenever I open my mouth, words may be given me so that I will fearlessly make known the mystery of the gospel. (Ephesians 6:19)

- And pray for us, too, that God may open a door for our message, so that we may proclaim the mystery of Christ, for which I am in chains. (Colossians 4:3)

"Pray for me." (part 2)

Jan Hus (c. 1369–1415) was a Czech religious thinker, philosopher, reformer, and professor. He also contributed to the development of the language of the Czechs, who still honor him as a national hero. His teachings were some of the most influential in history and served as a catalyst for the Protestant Reformation. He actively believed that people should be permitted to read the Bible in their own language.

Because of his views, Hus was imprisoned in a dark, murky dungeon. It was located where the sewers entered a lake. There he lay for almost three months. Within a few weeks he fell ill with a very high fever and was bothered by rheumatism, gallstones, and constant vomiting. Later, Hus was moved to another place of imprisonment, where he remained bound in chains night and day for seventy-three days. Writing from prison he had but one concern: "Dearly beloved! I entreat you, lying in prison, of which I'm not ashamed, for I suffer in hope for the Lord God's sake, to beseech the Lord God for me that He may remain with me."[2]

Recognize Your Need for Prayer

H. B. London Jr. is vice president in charge of ministry outreach and pastoral ministries for Focus on the Family. As a fourth-generation minister, he has an intimate understanding of the stresses and perils involved in ministry. Neil Wiseman is a church consultant who previously served as a pastor and professor of pastoral development. In their book *Pastors at Greater Risk*, they quote the startling statistics from research conducted by Fuller Theological Seminary:

- 80 percent of pastors say they have insufficient time with their spouse and that ministry has a negative effect on their family.
- 40 percent report a serious conflict with a parishioner once a month.
- 33 percent say that being in ministry is an outright hazard to their family.
- 75 percent report they've had a significant stress-related crisis at least once in their ministry.
- 58 percent of pastors indicate that their spouse needs to work either part-time or full-time to supplement the family income.
- 56 percent of pastors' wives say they have no close friends.
- 45 percent of pastors' wives say the greatest dangers to them and their family are physical, emotional, mental, and spiritual burnout.
- 21 percent of pastors' wives want more privacy.
- Pastors who work fewer than 50 hours a week are 35 percent more likely to be terminated.
- 40 percent of pastors have considered leaving the pastorate in the past three months.
- 25 percent of pastors' wives see their husband's work schedule as a source of conflict.
- 13 percent of pastors have been divorced.
- The clergy has the second-highest divorce rate among all professions.
- 48 percent of pastors think being in ministry is hazardous to family well-being.[3]

I know that you may not be a pastor, but regardless of where you serve in spiritual leadership, the pressures of ministry are intense. What do these statistics mean? They mean all spiritual leaders need prayer.

The Power of Prayer Partners in 1400 BC

A story from the life of Moses serves as a great picture of the importance and impact of the leader being supported by the prayers of his people. The Hebrews were being attacked by the Amalekites. Joshua was to lead the army out and fight while Moses was to stand on the hill holding up his staff, which symbolized God's power and victory.

The plan worked, until Moses' arms got tired. "So Joshua fought the Amalekites as Moses had ordered, and Moses, Aaron and Hur went to the top of the hill. As long as Moses held up his hands, the Israelites were winning, but whenever he lowered his hands, the Amalekites were winning" (Exodus 17:10, 11).

Fortunately, Moses had two men who took it upon themselves to hold up his hands. These unsung heroes were the difference between defeat and victory: "When Moses' hands grew tired, they took a stone and put it under him and he sat on it. Aaron and Hur held his hands up—one on one side, one on the other—so that his hands remained steady till sunset. So Joshua overcame the Amalekite army with the sword" (vv. 12, 13).

The point of this event is twofold: First, the people are only able to fully experience victory *as* their leader holds his or her hands up in prayer for them (1 Timothy 2:1). Second, leaders must be sustained through the prayers of their people.

E. M. Bounds was a successful lawyer, pastor, editor, and evangelist. He gave the last seventeen years of his life to prayer, rising every day without exception at 4 a.m. and praying until 7 a.m. During this period he wrote a series of classic books on prayer. Regarding the event recorded in Exodus 17, in a chapter titled "The Preacher's Cry: Pray for Us," Bounds wrote, "By common consent, this incident in the history of Israel has been recognized as a striking illustration of how people may sustain their preacher by prayer, and how victory comes when people pray for their preacher . . . We have a striking picture of the preacher's need for prayer, and of what a people's prayers can do for him."[4]

In his widely popular book *Power through Prayer* (1912), Bounds included a chapter titled "Preachers Need the Prayers of People." In it he stated, "Air is not more necessary to the lungs than prayer to the preacher. It is absolutely necessary for the preacher to pray. It is absolutely necessary for the preacher to be prayed for . . . the true apostolic preacher must have the prayers of other people to give his ministry its full quota of success."[5]

Peter Wagner wrote an entire book on the need for intercession to be made on behalf of spiritual leaders. The thesis of the book is very clear: "The most underutilized source of spiritual power in our churches today is intercession for Christian leaders."[6] If we hope to be the prevailing church Jesus predicted, we must pray for our leaders. If we hope to become the leaders our churches need us to be, we must train our people to pray for us.

The Power of Prayer Partners

In the First Century

In the early years of Christianity, the ruler of Israel was King Herod. In hopes of pleasing the Jews, Herod had the apostle James killed. Seeing how greatly this pleased the Jews, he then had Peter arrested as well. Things looked bleak, but Luke gives us insight to what happened behind the scenes: "So Peter was kept in prison, but the church was earnestly praying to God for him" (Acts 12:4, 5).

"But the church was earnestly praying to God for him." History reveals that when the church gets earnest in her prayers, things happen.

> The night before Herod was to bring him to trial, Peter was sleeping between two soldiers, bound with two chains, and sentries stood guard at the entrance. Suddenly an angel of the Lord

appeared and a light shone in the cell. He struck Peter on the side and woke him up. "Quick, get up!" he said, and the chains fell off Peter's wrists.

Then the angel said to him, "Put on your clothes and sandals." And Peter did so. "Wrap your cloak around you and follow me," the angel told him. Peter followed him out of the prison, but he had no idea that what the angel was doing was really happening; he thought he was seeing a vision. They passed the first and second guards and came to the iron gate leading to the city. It opened for them by itself, and they went through it. When they had walked the length of one street, suddenly the angel left him.

Then Peter came to himself and said, "Now I know without a doubt that the Lord sent his angel and rescued me from Herod's clutches and from everything the Jewish people were anticipating." (Acts 12:6–11)

The church prayed and things happened! You have to love the scene Peter's appearance must have created at the prayer meeting that night (vv. 12–17) and the commotion it caused in the prison the next morning (vv. 18, 19). Soon afterward, Herod ended up being eaten by worms (vv. 20–23)! On top of that, the Word of God spread and increased (v. 24). Wow! Intercessory prayer for a spiritual leader makes a difference.

In the Eighteenth Century

Jonathan Edwards (1703–1758) was a great American pastor, theologian, and revivalist. His sermon titled "Sinners in the Hands of an Angry God" is considered by many to be the catalyst of the Great Awakening. Apart from his theological and ministerial influences, Edwards also left a great legacy through his family. Many of Jonathan and Sarah Edwards' descendants became prominent citizens in the United States, including Vice President Aaron Burr and three Christian college presidents.

Edwards experienced and analyzed the nature of spiritual impact as few men have ever done. In speaking of the nature of revivals, he touted the necessity of prayer for spiritual leaders:

> If some of the Christians that have been complaining of their ministers . . . had applied themselves with all of their might to cry out to God for their ministers—had, as it were, risen and stormed heaven with their humble, fervent, and incessant prayers for them—they would have been much more in the way of success.[7]

If it be, as you have heard, the proper excellency of a minister of the gospel to be a burning and a shining light, then it is your duty earnestly to pray for your minister, that he may be filled with divine light, and with the power of the Holy Ghost, to make him so. For herein you will but pray for the greatest benefit to yourselves. For if your minister burns and shines, it will be for your light and life.[8]

In the Twenty-First Century

John Maxwell (1947–) had an effective ministry when he served as pastor of Skyline Wesleyan Church in San Diego, California. Incredible church growth occurred when lay involvement in ministry increased from 112 to 1,800 people. He attributes the success, in part, to two factors. First, God gave him a prayer partner. He writes, "I grew up in a Christian home where prayer was important. And as a pastor, I spent time in prayer every day. But it wasn't until God brought me a prayer partner that my life and ministry exploded with power, and the results began to multiply in an incredible way."[9]

Maxwell proceeds to tell how Bill Klassen, a gentleman about sixty years of age, sought him out to become his personal prayer partner and accountability partner. During his years at Skyline, Klassen's prayers made a difference.

The second factor in Maxwell's success was the prayer partner ministry he and Klassen organized at their church. The prayer partners were a group of people who: 1) prayed for John daily and 2) met in small groups in a tiny room at church every Sunday to cover the services with prayer. It began with thirty-one men and grew to include 120.

Max Lucado (1955–), the noted Christian author, is the longtime pastor of Oak Hills Church in San Antonio, Texas. Following Maxwell's example, he recruited 120 people who formed a prayer team. They covenanted to pray *for* him daily and pray *with* him fervently. Also, each Sunday one-fourth of them would arrive at church early and pray for the congregation. After just six months, Lucado enthusiastically assessed the results of the prayer partners' ministry:

> Has God honored the prayers of his people? Here is a sample of what God has done since we organized the Prayer Partners.
>
> We have broken our Sunday attendance record twice.
>
> We have finished the year with our highest-ever Sunday attendance.
>
> We have finished the year—hang on to your hat—over budget.
>
> We have added three new staff members and six elders.
>
> We witnessed several significant healings . . .
>
> Our church antagonism is down, and church unity is high.
>
> More significantly we called our church to forty days of prayer and fasting, inviting God to shine his face on his people. More than ever I'm convinced. When we work, we work; but when we pray, God works.[10]

"My people pray for me."

In London in the 1800s, Charles Spurgeon grew what was one of the largest megachurches since the first century, with ten thousand attending each week. He also founded a successful college and was a widely read and respected author. When asked the reason for his unusual success, Spurgeon often simply replied, "My people pray for me."[11] Another writer noted that part of the secret of Spurgeon's effectiveness could be traced to ". . . the prayers of an illiterate lay brother who set on the pulpit steps pleading for the success of the sermons."[12]

The Unsung Heroes

I have often read with amazement the accounts of the mighty revivals under Charles Finney (1792–1875). Entire towns were stirred by the winds of his revivals. It was said that 80 percent of those converted in his meetings stood the test of time. Often the presence and power of God was so intense in the communities he visited in central New York that people either repented or died. For example, one time the presence of God was so intense an entire mill was shut down with people weeping without Finney even speaking a word. A total of three thousand people were converted in that small town.

The unusual effectiveness of Charles Finney's ministry can be traced back to an unsung gallery of prayer partners. The two most notable were Abel Carey and Daniel "Father" Nash. Often they went a few days ahead of Finney to pray. They prayed with Finney in the daytime after he arrived, and usually interceded for him elsewhere during the meetings in the evenings.

Nash (1763–1837), who retired from the pastorate at age forty-eight in order to give himself totally to prayer for Finney's meetings, would often go quietly into towns three or four weeks in advance of a meeting. There he might gather three or four other Christians with him. In a rented room they'd start praying and crying out for revival. Of Daniel Nash, Finney later wrote:

> When I got to town to start a revival a lady contacted me who ran a boarding house. She said, "Brother Finney, do you know a Father Nash? He and two other men have been at my boarding house for the last three days, but they haven't eaten a bite of food. I opened the door and peeped in at them because I could hear them groaning, and I saw them down on their faces. They have been this way for three days, lying prostrate on the floor and groaning. I thought something awful must have happened to them. I was afraid to go in and I didn't know what to do. Would you please come see about them?"
>
> "No it isn't necessary," I replied. "They just have a spirit of travail in prayer."[13]

It is important to note that shortly after Nash's death, Finney retired from the taxing task of leading revivals.

"The secret is out."

As a revivalist, Charles Finney was known for the powerful way God used him to impact entire cities for Christ. He was a passionate practitioner and an ardent student of revivals and of the role prayer played in them. In observing the unusual spiritual effectiveness of another pastor, Finney felt he had discovered the secret:

> I once knew a minister who had a revival fourteen winters in succession. I did not know how to account for it till I saw one of his members get up in a prayer meeting and make a confession. "Brethren," said he, "I have been long in the habit of praying every Saturday night till after midnight for the descent of

the Holy Ghost among us. And now brethren," he began to weep, "I confess that I have neglected it for two or three weeks." The secret was out. The minister had a praying church.[14]

My Favorite Prayer Partner Story

After D. L. Moody's church burnt down in the great Chicago fire of 1871, he took what was to be a short, quiet study trip to England. While there a pastor recognized him and prevailed upon Moody (1837–1899) to preach at his church. He preached in the Sunday morning service and the people seemed indifferent to his words.

But the evening service was completely different. An observer stated, "At half-past six in the evening, it seemed, while he was preaching, as if the atmosphere was charged with the Spirit of God. There was a hush upon all the people, and a quick response to his words, though he had not been much in prayer that day, and could not understand it."[15]

After his message Moody asked for people who desired to become a Christian to stand. Hundreds did.

Assuming that they misunderstood his invitation, he said, "All of you who want to be Christians step into the inquiry room." Within seconds the room was packed and overflowing.

Again Moody tried to thin the ranks. He said that if they *really* wanted to become a Christian they needed to stand. Everyone did.

Moody then prayed for them and said that if they were *really* serious they needed to come back the next night.

Shockingly, more people came on Monday night than had been there on Sunday. The spontaneous revival lasted ten days with more than 400 making professions of faith and joining the church.

The Rest of the Story

Moody was wise enough to recognize that someone must have been praying. During those ten days, Moody kept inquiring until he found a bedridden girl named Marianne Adlard. She spent many hours a day interceding for her church.

Sometime prior, she had read an article about an American named D. L. Moody. After reading of Moody's dynamic ministry to the poor of Chicago, she ripped out the article and placed it under her pillow. She began to pray, "O Lord, send this man to our church."

On the Sunday that Moody just happened to speak at her church, her sister went home and said, "Whom do you think preached this morning?"

After Marianne failed to guess, her sister responded, "It was D. L. Moody of America."

"I know what that means," cried Adlard. "God has heard my prayers."[16]

The *Rest of* the Rest of the Story

It was November 15, 1978. It was one of the few times I have ever missed church. It was a Wednesday night and I was a college student. I had the flu and stayed in bed with a fever. Unable to sleep, I was reading Moody's biography. When I read the story of Adlard, God spoke to me. I got out of my bed and sank to my knees, asking God to show up in power at prayer meeting.

The next day, I wrote these words in the margin of my copy of Moody's biography: "Sick and stayed home from prayer meeting, so I prayed for revival. GOD ANSWERED! They had a one hour and twenty minute invitation [at church]. [Then as dorm mates returned from church] had an hour prayer meeting in my room afterward. GOD ANSWERED!"

One of the guys who lived across the hall had come bursting in the door from church. He was under deep conviction. He literally pulled me out of my bed onto my knees and begged me to pray for him. I led him to Christ right there. He is a pastor today. My room then filled up with young men. A spontaneous prayer meeting broke out with guys repenting of sin and recommitting their lives to Christ.

Intercession Makes a Difference Today

Nancy Pfaff, as a project in graduate school, surveyed 130 pastors, evangelists, and missionaries, each of whom was prayed for, fifteen minutes a day, by one of 130 trained intercessors for an entire year. About 89 percent of those surveyed said that the prayers had contributed positively to their ministry effectiveness. They reported increased effectiveness in the use of their gifts, a high response to their ministry, more discernment and wisdom from God, improved attitudes, better personal prayer lives, and heightened leadership skills. Her research also discovered that daily prayer was more effective than weekly or monthly prayer.

Of the 109 pastors being prayed for, 60 percent indicated that their churches grew as a result of reaching the unchurched. One pastor saw his church grow from 15 to 600.

Pfaff concluded, "There exists a tremendous reservoir of untapped prayer power in every church which can be affirmed, trained, and deployed to see the lost won, the apathetic revived, the 'backslider' restored, and the committed made more effective."[17]

How to Tap into the Power of Prayer Partners

I have two suggestions. First, ask God to give you someone you can pray *with* regularly. It could be your mate, an associate, or a friend. For example, when I was in college I made a pact to not go to bed on a weeknight until I had prayed with my roommate. Our prayer pact built unity and brought answers.

Second, I recommend that you develop a team of people to pray *for* you. As a pastor, I developed a team of twelve men to pray for me daily. This is what I did:

1. Prayed about which men to ask.
2. Sent a personal letter to them explaining my need to receive prayer and requesting that they come to a special Saturday breakfast meeting.
3. In the meeting, laid out the Biblical basis of prayer partners (Exodus 17; Acts 12; 1 Thessalonians 5:25; 2 Thessalonians 3:1; Romans 15:30; Ephesians 6:19; Colossians 4:3). I explained my personal need for prayer partners. I asked them to give me their prayer requests. I asked them to make a one-year commitment to:
   • Pray for our church, themselves, and their family every day.
   • Take a few minutes of extra time to pray for me one day a week.
   • Take a few minutes every Saturday night to pray for me.
   All twelve agreed! So we prayed together and for each other.
4. Every two weeks, met with them for Bible study and prayer. I would also share my prayer requests for the next two weeks.

That year went amazingly well. Our church grew more and baptized more people than the previous year. My health improved, as did my marriage and time with God. I called them my "Mighty Men," after David's mighty men of 2 Samuel 23. During a large men's gathering I publicly recognized them and gave each a rugged gray T-shirt, emblazoned with the words

Mighty Man
2 Samuel 23
Since 1998

I thought they would think it was corny. Surprisingly, they loved it.

I told the rest of the men that in order to get a "Mighty Man" T-shirt, they would have to make the one-year commitment. I quickly had a total of twenty-five "Mighty Men." It was another stellar year.

The next year, I recruited a team of fifty men to make a one-year commitment to pray for me daily. Several of them served on teams who would pray during the worship services every Sunday.

Because they were all guys, I used a football image to help them understand their importance. Again, it was corny, yet effective. I called them the offensive line and told them their job was to block the Enemy. I said, "I can't throw touchdowns if you don't block. As the quarterback I can not effectively do my job [throw 'the touchdown pass' (i.e., speak so people would get saved, or significantly changed)] if you don't do yours (block the Enemy with their prayers). Like the quarterback of an NFL team, I might receive more credit when things go well and more blame when things go poorly, but when someone gets saved or set free, we all will get championship rings in heaven."

I also told them intercessory prayer is reciprocal (see Job 42:10). When they prayed for God to bless my marriage, God not only blessed *my* marriage, he blessed *their* marriages. When they asked God to bless my kids, God not only blessed *mine*, he blessed *theirs*. When they lifted up *my* health, or finances, or ministry, God blessed *theirs*.

One of the things I miss most about being a pastor is my Mighty Men.

Why don't you tap the power of intercession to bring greater blessing into *your* ministry?

APPLICATION WORKSHEET

What are two or three key thoughts you want to remember from this chapter?

1.

2.

3.

Select the Christian leader(s) over you in authority or influence. Make a covenant to *pray for them* just as you would want to be prayed for. Write their name(s) below.

Ask God to give you a team of intercessors to *pray for you*. List the names of these potential prayer partners:

Plan how you will train, appreciate, and communicate with your prayer partners.

Write down the first three steps in your plan:

1.

2.

3.

CHAPTER 5

Turn Your Problems into Prayer

Too MANY good leaders burn out or wear out under the immense weight of spiritual leadership. Each month, up to two thousand pastors quit the ministry never to return.[1] Research of twenty-five years ago showed clergy dealing with stress better than most professionals. However, since 1980, studies in the United States show a sharp change. Recent studies describe an alarming spread of burnout among pastors. One study told that three out of four parish ministers (out of a sample of 11,500) reported severe stress causing "anguish, worry, bewilderment, anger, depression, fear, and alienation."[2]

In a recent Assemblies of God survey, 17 percent of those who responded said that quite often they were depressed to the extent it affected their ministry performance. Another 20 percent said they experienced this level of depression every two or three months.[3]

In the September/October 2000 edition of *Physician* magazine Dr. Walt Larimore, vice president of medical outreach at Focus on the Family, along with Rev. Bill Peel, reported that 80 percent of pastors and 84 percent of their spouses are discouraged or dealing with depression. Forty percent of pastors and 47 percent of their spouses say they are suffering from burnout. The norm among men in our country who are experiencing depression at any given time is about 10 percent. The norm among pastors is 40 percent.[4]

That's talking about pastors. What about all the overburdened lay leaders who quit as well? Many others remain in their positions, but they just go through the motions.

Every leader deals with pressures and problems. My pastor used to say that for the spiritual leader there are two bad days for every good one. For the leader, dealing with difficulties is part of the territory. In one sense, if there were no problems then leaders would be unnecessary.

Practice Spiritual Stewardship

In his forty years as leader, Moses certainly dealt with a plethora of predicaments and a ton of troubles. I struggle to fathom trying to lead a million whiny spiritual babies through a desert for even one year. I cannot imagine what it must have been like to feel a level of responsibility for their physical, material, and spiritual needs for *forty* years. It is hard for me to comprehend the weight of setting up a new nation from that motley, messy multitude of slaves—poor Moses.

As you read Exodus and Numbers, note the number of recorded times when the entire nation, like "spoiled babies," rose up on their heels and complained *to* Moses and *about* Moses. Seemingly, they leaped from one complaining crisis to another.

In the desert the whole community grumbled against Moses and Aaron. (Exodus 16:2)

So they quarreled with Moses and said, "Give us water to drink." (Exodus 17:2)

The rabble with them began to crave other food, and again the Israelites started wailing and said, "If only we had meat to eat!" (Numbers 11:4)

All the Israelites grumbled against Moses and Aaron, and the whole assembly said to them, "If only we had died in Egypt! Or in this desert!" (Numbers 14:2)

Now the people complained about their hardships in the hearing of the LORD, and when he heard them his anger was aroused. (Numbers 11:1)

Poor Moses. Think about it. His people were so incredibly frustrating they even tried the Lord's patience!

Yes, every leader deals with problems. The bigger issue is *"How will you deal with them?"* All the effective leaders described in this book, especially Moses, were skilled at high-level problem solving. Moses, as much as any other leader, was gifted at approaching his problems with prayer stewardship. What that means is this: Instead of carrying the problems around on his own shoulders, he repeatedly took his problems with God's people back to God.

This powerful leadership principle of prayerful stewardship is seen frequently in the story of Moses leading the people through the wilderness (for example see Exodus 17:4; Numbers 11:13, 14). But the entire concept is succinctly summarized at the end of Moses' prayer in Exodus 33, when he said, "Remember that this nation is your people" (v. 13).

"Your people." Too many good leaders burn out or wear out under the immense weight of spiritual leadership. Moses' solution to burnout was prayerful stewardship. Wisely, he did not carry the burdens on his own shoulders. He took the problems of God's people back to God in prayer.

I have learned that even though it is rarely the only solution, prayer can *always* be part of the solution to a difficult problem. For me, the more and better I pray, the less I worry.

Turn Problems into Prayer

Eight hundred miles away from his homeland, working for a non-believer, Nehemiah heard the heartrending news—Jerusalem lay in ruin and reproach. Even though he had risen to a lofty position of professional prestige, he had a tender heart toward God and the people of God. The negative news stirred his emotions and touched his heart. He wept, he mourned, he fasted, but he did not stop there. He also *prayed*. "When I heard these things, I sat down and wept. For some days I mourned and fasted and prayed before the God of heaven" (Nehemiah 1:4).

Nehemiah turned problems into prayer. The next seven verses contain one of the loftiest, yet most powerful, prayers recorded in the entire Bible. But I believe that even more important than *what* he prayed was *that* he prayed, and that he prayed *before* he did anything else. Everything else in the book of Nehemiah was born out of that prayer.

Even though God's leaders tend to be men and women of action, the first response of high-impact leaders is prayer. Whenever he faced a crisis, Nehemiah first faced it on his knees. When the evil Sanballat tried to intimidate Nehemiah and his people, Nehemiah turned it into a prayer and went back to work (4:1–9). When his enemies tried to trick and dishearten him, Nehemiah prayed for strength (6:1–9). When they sent another man to attempt to discourage him and get him to flee for his life, he refused, prayed, and finished the work (6:10–15).

Of course it is best to pray before problems are even on the horizon, but often that is not possible. Therefore, leaders must learn that when troubles do arrive to pray, pray first, and pray until you either know what to do next or have peace that God has it all under control.

Like Moses before him, Nehemiah took his troubles to God. Effective spiritual leaders turn their problems into prayer. They also turn their pressures into prayer.

Turn Pressures into Prayer

In the Gospels there are fifteen accounts of Jesus praying. Eleven are found in Luke's gospel. Why? The answer is that of the four gospel writers, Luke focused most on the *human* aspect of Jesus. Of course Jesus was fully God, but he was also fully man. Luke wanted us to see that as a *human* leader, Jesus lived a life of prayer. Since Jesus, the human, needed to pray, how much more do you and I?

Jesus Dealt with Daily Pressures in His Daily Prayer Time

As we studied in chapter 2, Jesus turned the daily pressures of high-octane ministry into daily morning prayer: "Very early in the morning, while it was still dark, Jesus got up, left the house and went off to a solitary place, where he prayed" (Mark 1:35).

Please note that Jesus did not simply enjoy a pleasant, early-morning time of prayer and then go back to bed. Mark's gospel tells us that Jesus used his morning season of prayer as the launching pad for another full day of ministry.

> Simon and his companions went to look for him, and when they found him, they exclaimed: "Everyone is looking for you!"
>
> Jesus replied, "Let us go somewhere else—to the nearby villages—so I can preach there also. That is why I have come."
> So he traveled throughout Galilee, preaching in their synagogues and driving out demons. (Mark 1:36–39)

In reflecting on what this daily prayer time meant to Jesus, S. D. Gordon observed, "Prayer wonderfully clears the vision; steadies the nerves; defines duty; stiffens the purpose; sweetens and strengthens the spirit. The busier the day for Him, the more surely must the morning appointment be kept. And an even earlier start made, apparently."[5]

Jesus Faced Crushing Pressure on His Knees

No human ever had to deal with more pressure than Jesus Christ. He had to live a life and die a death that would ultimately save the world from sin.

The greatest tension Jesus faced surrounded his crucifixion. It loomed before him. For a year, he had repeatedly predicted his crucifixion (Matthew 12:40; 17:9, 12, 22; 20:18; 27:63; Mark 9:12, 31; Luke 17:25; 18:32; 24:7; John 2:19). The horrors awaiting him on the cross stretched out before him. He realized he would soon be arrested, tried, beaten, and killed. He knew he was about to experience some of the greatest physical torture available in the first century. On top of that would be the emotional anguish of being betrayed by his disciples, abandoned by his friends, scorned by the religious leaders, and rejected by the crowd.

Yet, most awful of all, Jesus realized he was about to face a nightmare worse than any human had ever or would ever endure. The sinless Son of God, for the first time in eternity, would experience sin.

Imagine all the sins of all the people of all time were to be poured out on him. Beyond that, as the worst sinner ever, Jesus would face the righteous wrath and just judgment of God, his Father, as the sin was punished. In the awful hours after the Last Supper and just prior to his arrest, the emotions he endured were overwhelming.

Ironically, and symbolically, Jesus went to the Mount of Olives to a place called Gethsemane. The word *Gethsemane* means "the oil press," as large wooden presses were used to crush the oil from the olives. In a similar way Jesus faced the crushing pressure of his looming crucifixion.

How did Jesus deal with such intense stress and pressure? He turned it into prayer:

Jesus went out as usual to the Mount of Olives, and his disciples followed him. On reaching the place, he said to them, "Pray that you will not fall into temptation." He withdrew about a stone's throw beyond them, knelt down and prayed, "Father, if you are willing, take this cup from me; yet not my will, but yours be done." An angel from heaven appeared to him and strengthened him. And being in anguish, he prayed more earnestly, and his sweat was like drops of blood falling to the ground. (Luke 22:39–44)

I doubt that any of us can grasp the extent of what Jesus endured. The stress of what he was facing resulted in sweat like drops of blood dripping from his forehead. How did he survive it? He knelt down and prayed.

If Jesus felt the need to turn his crushing pressures and problems into prayer, how much more should you and I?

Cry for "Help!"

David was also a leader who dealt with immense pressure. As a young man he faced a murderous giant—literally! Then when all seemed to be going well, he was nearly killed by his king and was forced to flee his home and family, spending years as a fugitive, the most hunted man in the history of Israel. During this time and through his early years as king, he had to repeatedly fight the barbaric Philistines. Even after being king many years, he had the embarrassing stress of being forced to abandon his throne when his own son launched a military coup against him.

When you study his prayers, one thing is quite telling. David's most used prayer by far was not flowing and eloquent. It was short and blunt. In fact, it only encompassed one word—"Help!" Again and again, David ran to God crying for help (emphasis added):

Listen to my cry for **help**, my King and my God, for to you I pray. (Psalm 5:2)

Help, LORD, for the godly are no more; the faithful have vanished from among men. (Psalm 12:1)

In my distress I called to the LORD; I cried to my God for **help**. From his temple he heard my voice; my cry came before him, into his ears. (Psalm 18:6)

But you, O LORD, be not far off; O my Strength, come quickly to **help** me. (Psalm 22:19)

Hear my cry for mercy as I call to you for **help**, as I lift up my hands toward your Most Holy Place. (Psalm 28:2)

O LORD my God, I called to you for **help** and you healed me. (Psalm 30:2)

Hear, O LORD, and be merciful to me; O LORD, be my **help**. (Psalm 30:10)

In my alarm I said, "I am cut off from your sight!" Yet you heard my cry for mercy when I called to you for **help**. (Psalm 31:22)

Come quickly to **help** me, O LORD my Savior. (Psalm 38:22)

Hear my prayer, O LORD, listen to my cry for **help**; be not deaf to my weeping. (Psalm 39:12)

Be pleased, O LORD, to save me; O LORD, come quickly to **help** me. (Psalm 40:13)

I have done no wrong, yet they are ready to attack me. Arise to **help** me; look on my plight! (Psalm 59:4)

Save us and **help** us with your right hand, that those you love may be delivered. (Psalm 60:5)

I am worn out calling for **help**; my throat is parched. My eyes fail, looking for my God. (Psalm 69:3)

Hasten, O God, to save me; O LORD, come quickly to **help** me. (Psalm 70:1)

Save us and **help** us with your right hand, that those you love may be delivered. (Psalm 108:6)

Help me, O LORD my God; save me in accordance with your love. (Psalm 109:26)

Maybe you are not sure how to pray or what to say. You can always pray what David prayed. You can always cry out to God for HELP!

"Help!" (part 2)

Everything was going great for Judah and good king Asa, until the day trouble stormed up from Egypt. Asa's trouble was spelled Z-E-R-A-H. Zerah was the Ethiopian warlord who led a massive war machine of one million troops *and* three hundred chariots. Asa was outnumbered by four hundred thousand skilled troops and had no defense against the devastating speed and power of the chariots. It would be a massacre.

It was . . . for Zerah.

You see, Asa was a very effective spiritual leader. He practiced spiritual stewardship and turned his problems into prayer: "Then

Asa called to the LORD his God and said, 'LORD, there is no one like you to help the powerless against the mighty. Help us, O LORD our God, for we rely on you, and in your name we have come against this vast army. O LORD, you are our God; do not let man prevail against you'" (2 Chronicles 14:11).

What an excellent pattern for effective prayer! The whole prayer is short—only twenty-seven words in Hebrew. It contains everything necessary and nothing else. His prayer opened with appropriate words of praise: "LORD, there is no one like you to help the powerless against the mighty." Praise positions us to pray. He stated the petition clearly and succinctly: "Help us, O LORD our God."

Asa also gave God the reasons he expected God to answer. First, Judah was depending on God, not on themselves or anyone else: "for we rely on you." Second, Judah was representing God in this cause: "in your name we have come against this vast army." Third, Judah belonged to God and was allied with God: "O LORD, you are our God." Fourth, ultimately the battle was the Lord's: "do not let man prevail against you."

Asa's cry for "Help" worked and then some. God gave him a miraculous, exceedingly abundant, above-all-he-asked-or-thought answer:

> The LORD struck down the Cushites before Asa and Judah. The Cushites fled, and Asa and his army pursued them as far as Gerar. Such a great number of Cushites fell that they could not recover; they were crushed before the LORD and his forces. The men of Judah carried off a large amount of plunder. They destroyed all the villages around Gerar, for the terror of the LORD had fallen upon them. They plundered all these villages, since there was much booty there. They also attacked the camps of the herdsmen and carried off droves of sheep and goats and camels. Then they returned to Jerusalem. (2 Chronicles 14:12–15)

Spread It Out before the Lord

Two hundred years after Asa, it was nearly the same story with different characters. King Hezekiah's situation was very similar to Asa's, except his nemesis was Assyrian King Sennacherib. Like Zerah, Sennacherib also had a massive army and mighty chariots. He was on an undefeated run, wreaking havoc and destruction on the nine nations surrounding Judah from Lebanon to Egypt. Now it was Judah's turn to be crushed.

Sennacherib sent Hezekiah a letter calling for unconditional surrender. The Jews could choose to become slaves to the Assyrians or they would be slaughtered. What would you do if you faced such a dire dilemma?

Hezekiah did what effective spiritual leaders have done throughout the ages. He practiced spiritual stewardship and turned his problems into prayer: "Hezekiah received the letter from the messengers and read it. Then he went up to the temple of the LORD and spread it out before the LORD" (2 Kings 19:14).

Notice carefully the last six words of verse 14: "spread it out before the LORD." Hezekiah took Sennacherib's letter and went up to the temple of the Lord. There he spread it out before the Lord in prayer. That is the wise way for a spiritual leader to deal with his problems.

Look at what happened: "That night the angel of the LORD went out and put to death a hundred and eighty-five thousand men in the Assyrian camp. When the people got up the next morning—there were all the dead bodies!" (2 Kings 19:35).

When Sennacherib woke up and saw what had happened, he was so shook up that he and what was left of his army packed up and marched straight home. God did not like Sennacherib's arrogance—he *did* like Hezekiah's prayer.

All that was left for King Hezekiah's soldiers to do was collect the booty that the Assyrians had left behind in their hasty retreat.

Hezekiah had turned the problem over to God. God fought their battle and decisively won.

Cast Your Cares

Late in life, David had more than a problem. He had a painful, ugly, horrible, awful, massive, miserable mess. Unresolved family conflicts were boiling over and threatened to topple his rule. David's own son, Absalom, conspired against his leadership. Rumors, false reports, and slander were running rampant through Jerusalem. As a father, David couldn't fight his own son, but as the king, he couldn't merely sit still, either.

What could he do?

David used one of his best leadership tools and displayed a great secret of his leadership—he turned the problem into prayer. Psalm 55 is that prayer. Here are some highlights:

> Listen to my prayer, O God, do not ignore my plea; hear me and answer me. My thoughts trouble me and I am distraught. (vv. 1, 2)

> Destructive forces are at work in the city; threats and lies never leave its streets. If an enemy were insulting me, I could endure it; if a foe were raising himself against me, I could hide from him. But it is you, a man like myself, my companion, my close friend, with whom I once enjoyed sweet fellowship as we walked with the throng at the house of God. (vv. 11–14)

> But I call to God, and the LORD saves me. Evening, morning and noon I cry out in distress, and he hears my voice. He ransoms me unharmed from the battle waged against me, even though many oppose me. (vv. 16–18)

Cast your cares on the LORD and he will sustain you; he will never let the righteous fall. (v. 22)

"Call to God," "Cry out," "Cast all your cares on the LORD and he will sustain you." That was David's plan. Turn the problems into prayers. Cast the cares on the Lord. Let him sustain you.

Cast Your Cares (part 2)

The apostle Peter also knew about pressures and problems. He endured the trial of self-sabotage when he denied Jesus three times. He endured the pressure of fierce persecution. He experienced the growing pains of a growing ministry.

How did he deal with pressure and problems? He turned them into prayer.

For example, after Peter, on his way to the temple, had healed the crippled beggar, both he and John were arrested and brought before the same men who had decided to crucify Jesus. They were questioned and threatened before being released. What was their response? "On their release, Peter and John went back to their own people and reported all that the chief priests and elders had said to them. When they heard this, they raised their voices together in prayer to God" (Acts 4:23, 24).

When the church experienced the growing pains from exploding in numbers, Peter and the others came up with a plan. They would refuse to be defeated by the tyranny of the urgent. Instead they would delegate some of their administrative responsibilities in order to maintain the priority of prayer: "We will turn this responsibility over to them and will give our attention to prayer and the ministry of the word" (Acts 6:3, 4).

Later when Peter was writing to his scattered and persecuted flock, he also addressed the elders. Imbedded in his advice was his secret for overcoming the stress and anxiety of ministry: "Cast all your anxiety on him because he cares for you" (1 Peter 5:7). In other words, turn your pressures and problems into prayer.

Use Worry Lists

Martin Luther summarized the key to overcoming anxiety in five powerful words—"Pray and let God worry."[6] The apostle Paul gave the Philippians advice similar to that given by Luther and Peter when he wrote, "Do not be anxious about anything, but in everything, by prayer and petition, with thanksgiving, present your requests to God. And the peace of God, which transcends all understanding, will guard your hearts and your minds in Christ Jesus" (Philippians 4:6, 7).

One way I deal with the stress of leadership is to make worry lists. I make a list of the things I have coming for the day, a list of what is on tap for the rest of the week, and another list for the next two weeks. Then I turn my worry list into a prayer list and give each item to God.

Turn Prayers into Provisions

As a young leader, George Müller had a problem. He was responsible for the care and feeding of all the children in two orphanages. One day, there was no food in either house with no prospects on the horizon.

What did he do? He turned his problems into prayer. He called his workers together for a day of prayer. During the morning prayer meeting, two-thirds of the needed money for food was delivered unexpectedly by three separate individuals. When they met later in the day for prayer, they were interrupted by a knock at the door. There stood a messenger, and the rest of the need and then some was provided for.[7]

The practice of turning problems into prayer stuck with Müller. The larger the problem, the more frequent and ardent were his prayers and the greater the provision. Each time he faced a need, prayed for help, and saw God answer, his faith grew. Eventually he was feeding several thousand orphans a day, by prayer and faith.

As a result, God always met the need. More than once, a wagon pulled up to the door loaded with unexpected food, or there was a knock at the door with an unanticipated supply of food or the money to purchase all that was needed. Over and over, again and again, Müller and his staff turned their problems into prayers, which the Lord turned into provisions. Of the amazing way God provided the "daily bread" for the orphanages in answer to Müller's prayers, his biographer writes, "Throughout all his experience in conducting the orphanages this servant of God testifies that no meal, even when he was feeding two thousand orphans daily by faith, was more than thirty minutes late."[8]

To read Müller's biographies or his narratives of answered prayers is to read story after story of miracles. He deeply understood and practiced spiritual stewardship, prayer, and faith. He wrote, "We let God work for us, when the hour of trial of our faith comes, and do not work a deliverance of our own."[9]

Turn Problems into Rescue

D. L. Moody and his son William were on the German steamer *Spree* when it left Southampton, England, bound for New York on November 23, 1892. Three days and about 1,100 miles out to sea, sometime after midnight in the early morning hours of Saturday, November 27, the main propeller shaft broke. Two large fragments exploded through the bottom of the steamer. Immediately water filled half the ship's compartments and the pumps could not pump the water out as fast as it flowed in. The boat drifted for hours with no electricity, leaving the passengers terrified in the dark as the ship began to slowly sink.

At daybreak Moody beckoned the captain to join him and Will in prayer. Moody knelt down and prayed, "O Lord, when

Thy disciples were on the sea and in trouble, Thou didst save them. Are we not Thy disciples? Please smooth the waves so that we shall not be drowned, and please send us a ship."[10]

By Sunday morning all hope was lost, as the slowly sinking ship had now drifted off the course from where the other ships passed. Moody asked to hold a religious service for the passengers and crew. All attended except those crewmen needed at their posts. They sang and prayed.

At three o'clock Monday morning, Will woke Moody with good news. A light was visible in the distance rapidly approaching the *Spree*. It turned out to be the Canadian freighter *Lake Huron*, which towed the wounded *Spree* to safety.

Turn Indecision into Breakthrough

In his autobiography, *Just As I Am*, Billy Graham tells how prayer was the key to one of the biggest decisions in his ministry. He was concluding his 1949 crusade in Los Angeles. It had been a good, but unspectacular, set of meetings, and he felt an urge to extend the crusade. He writes:

> We needed a clear sense of direction from the Lord. Grady, Cliff, Bev, and I prayed together over and over again as the last week wore on. At last we decided to follow the example of Gideon in the Old Testament and put out a fleece, asking God to give us a decisive sign of His purpose.
>
> It came at four thirty the next morning.[11]

Stuart Hamblen (1908–1989), a popular entertainer to whom Graham had been witnessing, called on the telephone, broken and in tears. As the team prayed, Graham led Hamblen to Christ, giving them the answer about continuing the campaign.

The extended crusade exploded in popularity when Hamblen shared his testimony and the national media picked up the story.

The Graham campaign was a media sensation. Extraordinary conversions occurred. Celebrities began coming to the meetings and gave their lives to Christ. The meetings were extended week after week as the size of the crowd and the numbers responding to the invitation continued to grow.

The L.A. Crusade forever changed the size and scope of Graham's ministry. He writes, "All I knew was that before it was over, we were on a journey from which there would be no looking back."[12]

Again the team prayed for direction as to whether or not to extend the meetings. Again God responded. A fierce storm was heading toward Los Angeles from the Pacific. If it hit the coast it would no doubt wreak havoc with the huge tent used to hold the thousands attending the meetings each night.

This time the prayer fleece was that if God wanted them to continue, the storm would not reach Los Angeles. The next morning the newspapers reported that the storm had surprisingly dissipated at sea before hitting Los Angeles.

Organized prayer meetings for the campaign were being held all over Southern California and even across the United States:

> Students were praying in Christian colleges, businesspeople were praying in offices, families were praying in their homes, and congregations were gathered for special prayer meetings . . . "the mightiest force in the world," as Frank Laubach called prayer, undergirded me and brought the blessing of God from Heaven to Los Angeles.[13]

Because of prayer, God did many miracles during that eight-week campaign. Thousands accepted Christ as their Savior; 82 percent of them had never been church members. On top of that, the entire nation had been touched. In retrospect Graham wrote:

> Overnight we had gone from being a little evangelistic team . . . to what appeared to many to be the hope for national and

international revival. Everywhere we turned, someone wanted us to come and do for them what had been done in Los Angeles. What they didn't know however, was that we had not done it . . . Whatever this could be called and whatever it would become, it was God's doing . . . That was the whole secret of everything that happened: God had answered prayer.[14]

"God had answered prayer." That was the secret of Billy Graham's success. It can also be the secret of yours. Turn your problems into prayer.

APPLICATION WORKSHEET

What are two or three key thoughts you want to remember from this chapter?

1.

2.

3.

Make a list of your biggest concerns or the big, God-sized impossible problems you or your ministry are currently facing.

Prayerfully cast each one on the Lord.

CHAPTER 6

Fast and Pray

FASTING HAS long played a significant role in the prayer ministry of the effective spiritual leader. Great leaders know what it is to feel the burden of the Lord and hear him call them away into extended seasons of fasting and prayer. The Bible and history are littered with examples of the power of prayer and fasting to turn the tide and make the difference.

It was after forty days of fasting that Moses came down from Mt. Sinai with the Ten Commandments and a face that radiated the glory of the Lord (Exodus 34:27–29).

Samuel fasted and cried out to the Lord, and God gave Israel a thunderous (literally) victory over the Philistines (1 Samuel 7:5–11).

Jehoshaphat led his nation in fasting and prayer, and as a result they experienced a complete deliverance and miraculous victory (2 Chronicles 20:2–26).

God promised to reverse the plight of his people if they would repent (Joel 2:12–27). In response, King Josiah proclaimed a fast (Jeremiah 36:9).

Ezra called a fast, and as a result the pilgrims were able to travel safely from Babylon to Jerusalem (Ezra 8:21–23).

As a result of Esther's instructions to fast, the Jews living under Persian rule had their fortunes wonderfully reversed as they were unexpectedly delivered and prospered (Esther 4:16–10:3).

Even the wicked city of Nineveh received deliverance when they turned to God with fasting (Jonah 3:1–10).

Other leaders such as David, Elijah, Ezra, and Daniel discovered the power available to those who cry out to God through fasting. They are not alone.

After having fasted forty days, Jesus resisted the devil's temptations and launched his ministry in the power of the Spirit (Luke 4:1–14).

Frequent fasting marked the powerful prayer life of the apostle Paul (Acts 9:9; 2 Corinthians 6:5; 11:27).

For centuries early church leaders fasted twice every week. Epiphanius (c. 315–403), who authored what could be considered the first Christian encyclopedia, asked rhetorically, "Who does not know that the fast of the fourth and sixth days of the week (Wednesday and Friday) are observed by Christians throughout the world?"[1]

Augustine (354–430), the seminal theologian whose views deeply etched Christian thought, had a simple, yet significant, opinion of fasting: "Fasting is a Christian duty."[2]

The giants towering over church history were leaders who have practiced the spiritual discipline of prayer with fasting. Martin Luther, the father of the Protestant Reformation, learned fasting during his formative years as a monk. Later he taught that while fasting is no substitute for saving faith in Christ, it is a powerful tool for sanctification and a godly weapon in spiritual warfare.[3]

John Calvin, long considered one of the most influential leaders and theologians in history, habitually fasted. He viewed fasting as a necessary aid to the earnestness and fervency of his prayers.[4]

Other influential leaders such as John Knox, Jonathan Edwards, Charles Spurgeon, D. L. Moody, Charles Finney, Bill

Bright, and Billy Graham were all practicing proponents of prayer and fasting.

A Glorious Day

History views John Wesley as an inspiring preacher, wise organizer, relentless social activist, challenging writer, historic church builder, and world-shaking reviver. The man rode 250,000 miles on horseback, preached 40,000 sermons, gave away £30,000, and left a legacy of 132,000 followers. He also was a strong advocate for fasting.

As a young man, leading the Holy Club, or Methodists, of Oxford, Wesley followed the pattern of the early church and fasted two days a week, Wednesdays and Fridays. Later in life, his Friday fast was conducted according to the Jewish "day," which stretched from sundown to sundown. Therefore, from the end of each Thursday evening meal until late afternoon Friday, Wesley gave himself to fasting and prayer.

As a leader, he expected all his "preachers" to participate in fasting. In fact, he wanted all the Methodist leaders and people to follow this discipline.

Wesley also observed fasting on other days as situations dictated. He tells us in his journal of national deliverance in England in 1756 that the king of Britain called for a day of solemn prayer and fasting because of a threatened invasion by the French. Wesley wrote, "The fast day was a glorious day, such as London has scarce seen since the Restoration. Every church in the city was more than full, and a solemn seriousness sat on every face. Surely God hears prayer, and there will yet be a lengthening of our tranquility."[5]

In a footnote in his journal, Wesley later added, "Humility was turned into national rejoicing for the threatened invasion by the French was averted."

Biblical Fasting

Fasting as used in the Bible means "not to eat" or "self-denial." In the Old Testament the word *fast* is derived from the Hebrew term *tsom*, which refers to the practice of self-denial. In the New Testament, the Greek word is *nestia*, which also refers to self-denial. A summary of the biblical teaching on fasting reveals it to be choosing not to partake of food because spiritual hunger is so deep, determination in intercession is so intense, or spiritual warfare is so demanding that you temporarily set aside even fleshly needs to give yourself more wholly to prayer.[6]

A normal fast involves fasting from all food, but not from water (Matthew 4:2). An absolute fast is very rare, and involves abstaining from food *and* water in the face of extreme spiritual emergency (Acts 9:9; Ezra 10:6; Esther 4:16; Deuteronomy 9:9, 18; Exodus 34:28; 1 Kings 19:8). Because the body needs fluids to survive, one would need to be very sure of the leading of God to undertake such a fast for any period longer than three days. A partial fast is the restriction of one's diet as opposed to complete abstention (Daniel 10:3). Fasting may also include skipping a meal consistently or abstaining from certain foods or other activities. Many of us would benefit from a media fast from television, movies, and the Internet.

Typically, biblical fasting went for one complete twenty-four-hour period, usually from sundown to sundown. As we previously mentioned, the early church fasted two days every week, Wednesday and Friday. Pharisees fasted Tuesday and Thursday. Other biblical fasts went from three to forty days.

In the Bible, there are both individual and corporate fasts. Corporate fasts could involve the whole church (Acts 13:1–4) or even the entire nation (Jonah 3; Esther 4; 2 Chronicles 20).

The early church also practiced fasting for several days prior to Easter. Later, this fast took the form of a series of one-day fasts each week for the weeks leading up to Easter. It was also customary for Christians in the post-apostolic period to fast in preparation for their baptism.[7]

Why Fast?

Several years ago I read through the Bible, studying every passage regarding fasting. I started out looking for benefits of fasting. But, soon the question in my mind changed from "Why fast?" to "Why don't I fast more often?"

Working chronologically, I discovered twenty significant blessings gained by those who fasted in the Bible:

1. Fasting held back God's judgment. Moses fasted forty days to be able to intercede with God on behalf of the Israelites after they had sinned with the golden calf. God heard and spared the nation of Israel (Deuteronomy 9:18–26).
2. Fasting gave Hannah a stunning answer to prayer (1 Samuel 1:7). Even though she had long been barren, she conceived a special son, Samuel, who would shake a nation with his prayers.
3. Fasting brought about unexpected victories. For example, Israel was being pummeled by the Benjamites at Gibeah, losing twenty-two thousand men one day and eighteen thousand the next. Then they fasted, the Lord fought on their side, and the next day they lost only thirty men, while their enemies suffered 25,100 casualties (Judges 20:26, 35)! Years later, Israel was surrounded by the Moabites, Ammonites, and Meunites and faced certain defeat. The whole nation fasted and prayed and defeated them all without losing a man (2 Chronicles 20:3, 4, 12, 15).
4. David humbled himself through fasting. He advocated fasting as a means to empathize with a sufferer and develop humility (Psalm 35:13; 69:10).
5. Fasting provided God's protection. Ezra and the rest of the remnant who returned from exile to rebuild the temple had

no one to protect them as they traveled. They fasted and prayed, and God protected them (Ezra 8:21–23).

6. Fasting yielded a plan and provision. Jerusalem lay in ruin and reproach. She desperately needed her walls repaired so the rest of the city could be protected and rebuilt. Nehemiah fasted and prayed, and God gave him the plan for accomplishing the seemingly impossible job (Nehemiah 1:4).

7. Fasting rescued a nation. The Jews faced extinction as a plan was hatched and the king of Persia was being coerced to exterminate the Jews. Yet, Esther and her people fasted and prayed. God not only spared the Jews, he elevated their leaders (including Esther) *and* destroyed the ones seeking their slaughter (Esther 4:3–16).

8. Fasting has the power to please God by loosing the chains of injustice, setting the oppressed free, and providing for the hungry, the homeless, and the naked; it causes righteousness to shine, healing to come, and God's glory to surround you. It leads to answered prayer (Isaiah 58:6–14).

9. Fasting purifies soul and body. Daniel fasted from pagan delicacies and was rewarded with better health and increased favor (Daniel 1).

10. Fasting made it possible to receive revelation from the Lord. For Daniel, fasting brought the revelation of the great prophecy of the seventy weeks. For us, it can aid in the understanding of such prophecies (Daniel 10:2, 3).

11. Fasting brought a nation back to God (Joel 2:12).

12. Fasting prepares for the return of Jesus, the Bridegroom (Joel 2:15–18; Luke 2:57; 5:33–35).

13. Fasting is a powerful expression of repentance. The wicked city of Nineveh would have been destroyed without her repentance and fasting (Jonah 3:5–9).

14. Fasting is a secret service to God, often where deep heart desires are expressed. God, who sees in secret, promises to reward it openly (Matthew 6:4, 6, 18).

15. Fasting is a spiritual service. Anna, a widow in her eighties, served the Lord with fasting day and night (Luke 2:23, 37).

16. Fasting obeys the implied command of Jesus. In Matthew 6, he was correcting external acts of righteousness performed with wrong motives. When he came to the subject of fasting, he began by saying, "When you fast . . ." (Matthew 6:16–18). He did not say, "*If* you fast." For the serious follower of Jesus, fasting was not an option; it was an expectation. As we have already mentioned, the early church fasted two days a week and turned the world upside down. If we want their power, we need to follow their practices.

17. Fasting is a powerful aid in spiritual warfare. After his disciples failed to cast out a demon, Jesus did so easily. Then he explained, "This kind does not go out except by prayer and fasting" (Matthew 17:21). The validity of verse 21 is questioned by textual critics as possibly not having been in the original book of Matthew. Even if that is the case, it does not lessen the fact that it was the understanding of the early Christians that the bonds of oppression (Isaiah 58) placed on souls by demons are broken by prayer and fasting.

18. Fasting increases spiritual power and prepares for greater impact. Jesus experienced forty days of prayer and fasting. Immediately after that we see him preaching with the power of the Holy Spirit. Even though he was God, this power was not present in this way prior to his time of prayer and fasting for forty days in the wilderness (Luke 4:1–14).

19. Fasting aids decision making. The church at Antioch fasted and prayed prior to selecting Paul and Barnabas as missionaries (Acts 13:1–4). Later, Paul and Barnabas returned to places where they had previously started churches and selected leaders for those churches with prayer and fasting (Acts 14:23).

20. Daniel's twenty-one days of fasting and prayer were needed to aid the angel Gabriel in his assignment to deliver the answer

to Daniel's prayers (Daniel 9:3–10:3). If answers seem slow in coming without fasting, start praying *with* fasting.

Fasting Is . . .

Fasting is a great aid in building the spiritual life of a leader. After a forty-day fast, Liberty University cofounder and Vice President Elmer Towns (1932–) encountered God on a much deeper level. In his little book *Knowing God through Fasting,* Towns describes the spiritual benefits of fasting. For him, fasting was a means of:

1. Emptying yourself of every barrier to God so you can be filled with His presence.
2. Creating an appetite for the good things to follow.
3. Waiting in God's presence to become like Him and to do His will.
4. Coming to the Lord to enjoy His presence and find spiritual rest.
5. Drinking from God's presence to get spiritual satisfaction.
6. Disciplining yourself even as Jesus did.
7. Growing spiritually into the image of Jesus.
8. Gaining spiritual perception of God's world.
9. More than cessation of our activity, entering into God's rest.
10. Knowing God and becoming more like Him.[8]

Add Fasting

Wesley Duewel has given himself to the cause of missions for more than sixty-six years. Following nearly twenty-five years' ministry in India, he served as president of OMS (Oriental Missionary Society) for thirteen years. OMS is a pioneer missions agency in the area of training nationals, as seven thousand churches have been planted with a combined membership in excess of one million people in more than forty countries. About 1.7 million of

Duewel's books are now in circulation in sixty-one languages or national editions.

Duewel is an ardent believer in the unbreakable link between effective spiritual leadership and prayer, especially as prayer is wed with fasting. He writes:

> When you long to strengthen and discipline your prayer habits and to add a new dimension to your prevailing in prayer, add fasting. When you seek to humble yourself before God in total submission to His will and in total dependence on His almighty power, add fasting. When you face an overwhelming need, a human impossibility, and your soul hungers to see God intervene by supernatural power, add fasting.[9]

Four Big Requests

My first serious fast of more than one day was as a junior in college. I felt led to pursue a three-day fast with lots of intense prayer. I had four major requests that I needed or wanted to see answered in the following thirty days:

1. God would miraculously provide me with enough money to help some of my friends pay their school bills so they could stay in school.
2. I would lead fifty souls to Christ in the next month.
3. God would give me a mentor.
4. God would heal three students severely injured in an automobile accident.

Within thirty days the answers were coming in: All three students who were in the accident turned the corner, and we knew they would all live. One of my professors agreed to mentor me (although he did not follow through, I do believe God did *his* part). Unexpectedly, I received a check in the mail for $500, which was just enough to help several guys pay their school bills.

But it looked like the "fifty souls saved" was too much to expect. What was I thinking? I had no car and lived in a dorm with eighty Christian young men, on a mountain with only Christian students and teachers. Whom was I going to lead to Christ?

I did witness to the telephone repairman, and he prayed to accept Christ. I was asked to fill in as a last-minute replacement at a Christian haunted house. My job was to share the gospel at the end of the tour through the house. That weekend, twenty-one people prayed to accept Christ. That brought my total to twenty-two. That was amazing, but a very long way from fifty.

The last weekend of the month, I drove seven hours to speak at a youth retreat in a very remote part of southeastern Ohio. Several small churches had joined together and there were nearly 150 teens there. There were two other speakers, so I only had one chance to speak to the group.

I started my talk that night and it was going badly. To be honest, it was horrible.

So I stopped.

Out of nowhere, I got the idea to have everyone stand up, one by one, and rate themselves spiritually as either hot, cold, or lukewarm. Conviction settled on the group and the presence of God filled the room. After the first few students stood and rated themselves, teens started crying. Then kids got down on their knees. Soon everyone was on their knees. It went on for nearly an hour.

The ringleader of the unsaved, wild, rebellious kids fell on the floor and started shaking. Other kids started praying for him. He was unable to speak for half an hour. Then he came to his senses, got on his knees, and cried out to God to save him.

The next morning the pastor in charge of the retreat came up to me with a big smile on his face. "Twenty-eight!" he said.

"Twenty-eight what?" I asked.

"Twenty-eight kids gave their hearts to Christ last night," he said. "We have been fasting and praying for a breakthrough and God gave it to us last night. Twenty-eight kids got saved, and I mean saved. Most of them were the roughest kids at the high school. They have been bringing me cigarettes, alcohol, and pot all night, asking me to destroy it."

I smiled. *Thank God,* I thought. *He did an unusual work last night.*

Then it hit me. *Last night was the thirtieth day since my fast,* I thought. *Twenty-two people were saved before last night, twenty-eight more were saved last night. That makes fifty—not forty-nine, not fifty-one, but fifty. God answered all four of my impossible requests. Fasting made my prayers more effective."*

Fasting for Revival

I have read with eagerness accounts of the big moves of God in history. Almost all were clearly born out of fervent prayer and fasting. Let me give you some examples.

The revival movement that was born in New England in the early eighteenth century has been called the Great Awakening. In many ways, it began with a pastor named Jonathan Edwards and fasting. Burdened about the unconverted members of his church, Edwards fasted for twenty-two hours before giving his famous sermon "Sinners in the Hands of an Angry God."[10]

Several years later, in England, George Whitefield (1714–1770) and the Wesley brothers, John and Charles (1714–1770), were influenced by a praying group of Christian Moravians. Soon the three experienced what Whitefield later called "a Pentecostal season." Days and nights were spent praying and fasting. When these young men began to preach, they had such power that crowds swelled to hear their words. They soon took to preaching outside, where crowds numbered into the thousands.[11]

In this book, we have mentioned the revivals experienced under Charles Finney during the early 1800s. He and his co-laborers were intense prayer warriors who spent entire days fasting and praying. As a result, as many as a million people or more were swept into the kingdom of God. Some estimate 85 percent of professed converts in the Finney revivals remained true to the Lord.[12]

Not long after, during what is now called "the Laymen's Prayer Revival" in America, Christians fasted and prayed during their lunch hours as they attended noon interdenominational prayer meetings in churches near their places of employment. The meetings were informal, as anyone could pray, lead a song, or testify, with a five-minute limit placed on each.

They started in 1857 in New York City and soon these lunchtime prayer meetings spread to all the major cities of the Eastern seaboard. By May 1859, fifty thousand people had been converted to Christ through the prayer revival. Newspapers in New England reported that there were no unconverted adults in many towns![13]

Fasting for a Monetary Miracle

In 1971 Jerry Falwell started Liberty University. During its first twenty-five years of existence, Liberty grew rapidly from a handful of students to more than ten thousand in its various programs. Classroom buildings and dorms were built on a cash-only basis, with most of the money coming from supporters of Falwell's television program.

When scandals rocked the religious broadcasting world, contributions to every ministry, including Falwell's, decreased dramatically. But the university continued to grow and build. Soon the university was staring at more than $100 million in debt. Liberty risked losing its accreditation because of its excessive debt. The loss of accreditation would spell the end of the school. Falwell said, "With this crisis, I had to fast, and fast seriously."[14]

Falwell felt impressed by the Lord to go on a forty-day fast to pray for miraculous financial provision. He began July 20, 1997, and abstained from all food until September 1. He drank water, took a vitamin daily, and drank some vegetable juice every few days. The fast, however, did not go as he had planned:

> I kept asking God for money, but He impressed upon my heart that I needed to get close to Him, to listen to Him, and trust Him. When I asked for money, God told me not to ask for money, but to learn to know Him better. I had several lessons to learn before I could ask for money. As I ended that first forty-day fast, I felt I had learned what God wanted to teach me. But I did not have an answer about money.[15]

God is not an ATM into which we put prayer and/or fasting and automatically get back what we want. God is God. Falwell needed to learn that on a deeper level. Then he was ready to proceed. He said, "After resuming my normal diet for twenty-five days, God told me I could ask Him for money. So I went back on another forty-day fast that began September 25, 1996, ending on November 4."[16]

God responded.

First they received a huge cash gift that erased the long-term mortgage debt. Second, they got more money, which restored the university to financial health. Third, all accreditation sanctions were removed and accreditation was affirmed for the next decade.

I had lunch with Dr. Falwell a few months after that second fast and was impressed with his spiritual depth and humility. When asked about his fasts, he simply said, "Fasting is one of the great privileges of the Christian life. It is an act of self-denial that greatly enhances the power of our prayers."

During the last several years, answers from Falwell's fasts have continued to roll in. The university has continued to grow to more than ten thousand residential students *and* more than twenty thousand online distance learners. The facilities on campus have more than doubled, and financial health has been maintained.

Fasting for Healing and a Message to Preach to the World

Ronnie Floyd is a highly effective spiritual leader. In his twenty-plus years of ministry in Springdale, Arkansas, Pastor Floyd's church's membership has grown from 3,700 to more than 16,000 members. The church baptized more than 11,700 persons in his first twenty years.

In 1990 his wife, Jeana, was diagnosed with cancer. He began to fast and pray for her healing, usually one day a week, but sometimes two or three days at a time. As a result, she was completely healed.

In 1995, he felt led to pursue a forty-day fast for America and the church. His burden was to humble himself and seek God's face. Later he said, "God told me that during the forty-day fast He would give me a message to preach to the world."[17]

The answer came the next year when he was asked to address all the thousands of church leaders at the Southern Baptist Convention's annual gathering. Floyd preached with power and called on every church to fast and pray for revival. More than five thousand people came forward in response to the invitation. Others knelt and wept all over the arena. As a result, a letter was sent to the fifty thousand pastors of the SBC calling them to fast and pray. Along with the letter was a taped copy of Floyd's sermon and a booklet he had written titled *Gateway to Supernatural Power*. Copies were made and sent to missionaries around the globe. God had indeed given Floyd a message that was preached to the world.

Fasting for Huge Evangelistic Results

Bill Bright (1921–2003) was certainly one of the most effective spiritual leaders in history. His ministry, Campus Crusade for Christ, started in 1951 at the University of California–Los Angeles, has grown incredibly. Originally a ministry for college students,

Campus Crusade has expanded its focus to sixty different outreaches, including ministry to adult professionals, families, athletes, and high school students in 191 different countries. Today, Campus Crusade employs more than twenty-seven thousand full-time staff and has 225,000 trained volunteers.

Bright has been called the greatest evangelist of the twentieth century. His booklet *The Four Spiritual Laws* and Campus Crusade for Christ have reached astounding numbers of people around the world who have received Jesus Christ.

Bright was a man who deeply valued the power of prayer and fasting. He wrote his 1995 book *The Coming Revival: America's Call to Fasting and Prayer* with the purpose of recruiting two million people to join him in fasting and praying for forty days. He received in response to the book an incredible number of testimonies of what the Lord was doing as a result of fasting and prayer. In 1997, he wrote:

> I have been repeatedly moved and uplifted by these messages of answered prayers for spiritual growth, salvation for unsaved friends and family, physical healing, financial needs, release from sin, specific guidance, and a greater devotion to serve the Lord. Marriages have been restored, campuses awakened, and churches revived. God's power is indeed being poured out upon his people as a result of extended fasts to "seek God's face."[18]

Bright's lifelong passion was evangelism and discipleship in fulfillment of the Great Commission. In the wisdom of his later years, he ardently believed that the Great Commission would only be fulfilled when Christians experienced the transforming power of fasting. On his Web page devoted entirely to the power of prayer and fasting, he said:

> Fasting is the most powerful spiritual discipline of all the Christian disciplines. Through fasting and prayer, the Holy Spirit can

transform your life. Fasting and prayer can also work on a much grander scale. According to Scripture, personal experience, and observation, I am convinced that when God's people fast with a proper Biblical motive—seeking God's face not His hand—with a broken, repentant, and contrite spirit, God will hear from heaven and heal our lives, our churches, our communities, our nation and world. Fasting and prayer can bring about revival—a change in the direction of our nation, the nations of earth and the fulfillment of the Great Commission.[19]

Bright practiced what he preached by doing a forty-day fast annually from 1994 to 1998. When asked to describe the most significant results he personally experienced through prayer and fasting, he recalled many:

> The *Jesus* film was a vision I carried for 33 years before it became a reality in 1979. As of this date [1998], more than one billion three hundred million people have viewed the *Jesus* film in more than 440 languages. Tens of millions have received our Lord Jesus Christ.
>
> There has [sic] been many significant answers, but standing out in my mind are the great moves of God through the "I Found It" campaign and the gigantic EXPO gatherings of 1972, 1974, and 1985. Through these events, the Lord mercifully touched tens of thousands of lives.[20]

If Bright's claims of the power of fasting and prayer seem outlandish, consider this: The 1972 EXPO had eighty thousand in attendance, the 1974 event trained three hundred thousand in South Korea, and the "I Found It" campaign touched 85 percent of the people in America and led to 3.5 million people becoming Christians! By 2002, the *Jesus* film had been translated into 800 languages and had been viewed more than six billion times, resulting in untold numbers of decisions for Christ.

How to Fast More Effectively

Before You Begin

1. Determine from what and for how long you plan to fast. Will you be fasting for one meal, one full day, three days, or a week? Will you be abstaining from just solid food, or food *and* juice, or television, or the Internet, or the newspaper, or sweets?
2. Go through some of the reasons for fasting mentioned in this chapter and set some objectives for your fast.
3. Prepare yourself spiritually by repenting of any and every possible sin. Fasting cleanses your body while confession cleanses your heart.
4. Prepare yourself physically by cutting down to smaller meals a few days prior to beginning your fast. Especially prior to starting a fast of a week or more, start shrinking your stomach by eating smaller amounts. Don't gorge yourself with the last meal before you start fasting.
5. Try to plan to be less busy during the period you will be fasting. One of the goals is to be able to concentrate on God as much as possible.
6. Set aside ample time to spend with God.
7. Consider the effect fasting may have on your taking of prescription medications. Some things have to be taken with food. Can you skip a day or two? Can you take the medication with juice?

Other Practical Advice and Observations

1. Try to limit physical activities.
2. Drink a lot of liquid and expect to visit the facilities more frequently.
3. Be prepared for some headaches or joint pain as your body detoxifies. The headaches may be worse if you have been using large amounts of nicotine and/or caffeine.

4. Build up gradually. Start with one meal. The next time, go for a whole day. Then fast for three days. Then a week.
5. Most people can fast one to three days regardless of the busy-ness of their schedule.
6. You may tell others about your fast but do not boast.
7. The longer the fast, the more gradually it needs to be broken. Do not break a long fast with a heavy meal.

Still More Advice and Encouragement

1. If you have never fasted before, try it. You really have nothing to lose and much to gain.
2. You don't have to be a spiritual giant to fast. Remember, in the first few centuries of Christian history, most believers fasted two days a week.
3. Also, your fast does not have to be a forty-day fast to be effective. While many effective spiritual leaders have completed a forty-day fast, most haven't.
4. If you fast regularly, realize that most of the time, there is no immediate spiritual experience attached. Fasting is a spiritual discipline that allows God to transform you little by little, step by step as you humble yourself and seek his face.
5. Fasting is good for your body, but not necessarily easy. Physically, I generally feel lousy the first day or two of fasting. But in the days following, I feel great. I have more clarity and energy.
6. When you fast and pray you may want to ask God, "Please do *in* me what you *need* to do and do *for* me what you *want* to do."
7. Consider fasting one twenty-four-hour day a week, from sun-down one day to sundown the next day. That is the model practiced by the disciples.
8. Remember, the God who sees in secret will reward openly. Fasting is a secret service that can aid in bringing open answers to prayer.

APPLICATION WORKSHEET

What are two or three key thoughts you want to remember from this chapter?

1.

2.

3.

Do you believe that God is prompting you to fast?

How long do you think God would have you fast?

What do you think he wants you to abstain from during your fast?

What prayer requests are prompting your fast?

What are the objectives of your fast?

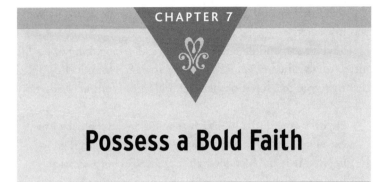

CHAPTER 7

Possess a Bold Faith

How WOULD you rate your prayers? Are they weak and wimpy, or strong and mighty? High-impact spiritual leaders pray differently than more common folks. They pray with greater boldness. They come to God with confident courage. They take seriously the promise of Hebrews 4:16: "Let us then approach the throne of grace with confidence, so that we may receive mercy and find grace to help us in our time of need."

When I say high-impact spiritual leaders pray boldly, I mean they evidence several earmarks of courageous faith in prayer. As you read about them, consider the level of boldness in *your* prayers.

Boldly Claim God's Promises

Transacting Business with God

Hudson Taylor was an Englishman who left a very deep mark for God both in China and around the world. From nothing, he founded the China Inland Mission, which at his death included 205 mission stations with more than 800 missionaries and 125,000 Chinese Christians.

Read that last sentence again slowly. How did he do it? What was his secret?

Taylor's son and daughter-in-law wrote a biography of his life interestingly titled *Hudson Taylor's Spiritual Secret*. In it they stated that there was one secret of the great impact of Hudson's leadership:

> He overcame difficulties such as few men have ever had to encounter, and left a work which years after his death is growing in extent and usefulness . . . largely as an outcome of this life, tens of thousands of souls won to Christ in previously unreached provinces . . . What was his secret? . . . the simple, profound secret of drawing for every need upon "the fathomless wealth of Christ."[1]

Where did Taylor learn this type of prayer life? The secret came from his sister, Amelia. He was converted, in part, through her persistent, prevailing prayers. She committed to give herself in prayer until he gave himself to Christ. The day she made her commitment, she wrote these words in her diary: "The promises of the Bible are very real, and prayer is in a sober fact transacting business with God, whether on one's behalf or on the behalf of those for whom one seeks blessing."[2]

Transacting business with God became a model for Hudson's dynamic life of bold faith and prayer. Every need, whether it was for funds, converts, or workers came by trusting God and claiming his promises.

The Future Is as Bright as the Promises of God

Another amazing pioneer missionary was an American named Adoniram Judson. He was a brilliant man, a highly capable lexicographer and Bible translator in Burma. He was a man who victoriously faced incredible odds because of his courageous faith in the promises of God.

With only his wife, Judson went as a pioneer into a land of millions where there was not one known Christian at that time. They labored six long, soul-crushing, heartbreaking years before their first convert came to Christ. Judson had to master the complex Burmese language without the aid of any textbooks. On the mission field, he suffered the untimely deaths of two wives, three children, and a number of coworkers. Judson was incarcerated for nearly two years in a squalid prison—emaciated, filthy, shackled, and hanging upside down much of the time. His few Burmese followers faced the constant threat of persecution. Still, Judson persevered in his work of preaching and translation.

How did he do it?

When he returned to Boston for his only furlough, Judson was asked by a prominent printer, "Do you think the prospects are bright for the speedy conversion of the heathen?"

Judson promptly replied, "As bright as the promises of God."

Amazingly, after his death a Burmese government survey recorded 210,000 Christians. Today there are nearly four million Burmese believers.

God's Checkbook

Charles Spurgeon was one of the leading lights of church history. Like other high-impact spiritual leaders, Spurgeon would fearlessly claim God's promises and quote them back to him. In his book *God's Checkbook: Daily Drawing on God's Treasury*, Spurgeon explains, "A promise from God may very instructively be compared to a check payable to order. It is given to the believer with the view of bestowing upon him some good thing. It is not meant that he should read it over comfortably, and have done with it. No, he is to treat it as a reality as a man treats a check."[3]

In his book, Spurgeon implores us to accept the promise personally "as one's own." After doing so, the believer must pray. "He must believingly *present* the promise to the Lord, as a man presents a check at the counter of the bank. He must plead it by prayer, expecting to have it fulfilled."[4]

In analyzing the secret of Spurgeon's incredible success in the ministry, one observer remarked regarding his "strong faith, and . . . intense earnestness."[5] Another confirmed this when he said, "It is not for nothing nowadays that one meets a man so desperately in earnest as he is."[6]

His biographer wrote, "His idea of prayer was passing over the counter a check bearing an honored name." For example, Spurgeon was dining with some friends when the discussion turned to the fact that the next morning Spurgeon needed to come up with a large sum to pay the builder of an orphanage. When asked about it, Spurgeon calmly said he had prayed about it and had confidence the money would come. As one of his friends was questioning Spurgeon's bold claim, they were interrupted by a messenger with a telegram. The telegram stated that someone had stopped by Spurgeon's church with a gift for the exact sum of money Spurgeon needed to pay the builder the next day.[7]

If We Don't Use His Promises to the Fullest, Then Christ Will Have Died in Vain.

When I was a college student my professor taught us that the greatest youth minister in history was a lady named Henrietta Mears (1890–1963). Never marrying, she had hundreds of "spiritual children." She became educational director at Hollywood Presbyterian in Southern California. Some of those she mentored included Dick Halverson, who became chaplain of the United States Senate, and Bill and Vonette Bright, who founded Campus Crusade for Christ.

Because of Henrietta's drive for souls, and ability to plan and prepare, the church grew to more than six thousand. Her own Sunday school class had as many as 500 university students and singles. Many of her church Bible study groups attracted businessmen and well-known movie stars to Christ. Needing strong biblical literature for hundreds of new believers, Henrietta began to write her own, and Gospel Light Press was born. She also started a conference center called Forest Home, which served as many as twenty-six thousand people a year.

One of Henrietta's biographers spent a great deal of time with her and discovered what she called "Miss Mears' secret":

> Her ministry has been a fast and furious search to find out the good things that God has promised to His children. She doesn't want to miss a promise and she doesn't want anyone else to miss one either. If I would present a caricature to describe Miss Mears it would be of her holding her Bible close to her eyes, her hands eagerly turning the pages, then pointing to a verse as she says in great delight and enthusiasm, "Here's another promise God has given us; oh, let's use this to the very fullest. Have you got one there? Well, let's use that one, too. Here's another promise! Let's claim this. If we don't use His promises to the fullest then Christ will have died in vain. Come on, young people, here is a glorious promise and I know it works! Here you are; take it, it's yours!"[8]

How to Claim Promises

Wesley Duewel claimed the promises of God as he served as a missionary in India and as the president of the massive OMS International missions agency. Today OMS includes seven thousand churches, with a combined membership in excess of one million people. Regarding the promises of God, Duewel wrote, "Promises to individuals have their first and primary significance for that person, but what God was willing to do for any Bible character He is eager to do for you when you have need."[9]

Can we claim the promises given to others in the Scriptures? Duewel says yes, under these conditions:

1. Study Scripture carefully to understand what is meant to those to whom it was originally given. Your spiritual application must be made in the light of this literal meaning.
2. Recognize that if this promise is God's promise to you, He will not only deeply impress it upon your heart, but will also provide corroborating evidence through providence, opinions of other Christians, and deep heart peace.
3. Keep your motive primarily for the glory of God, not your own self-interest, even though you may be benefited by the fulfillment of the promise.[10]

Promises of Answered Prayer

The Bible contains 7,487 promises. Many of these promises contain God's willingness to answer prayer. When we pray for things that we are confident God wants to do, we can boldly quote his Word back to him.

For example, Jesus gave his followers many promises in reference to answering our prayers. Some of my favorite promises regarding answered prayer include the following:

Ask and it will be given to you; seek and you will find; knock and the door will be opened to you. For everyone who asks receives; he who seeks finds; and to him who knocks, the door will be opened. Which of you, if his son asks for bread, will give him a stone? Or if he asks for a fish, will give him a snake? If you, then, though you are evil, know how to give good gifts to your children, how much more will your Father in heaven give good gifts to those who ask him! (Matthew 7:7–11)

Ask the Lord of the harvest, therefore, to send out workers into his harvest field. (Matthew 9:38)

I tell you the truth, if anyone says to this mountain, "Go, throw yourself into the sea," and does not doubt in his heart but believes that what he says will happen, it will be done for him. Therefore I tell you, whatever you ask for in prayer, believe that you have received it, and it will be yours. (Mark 11:23, 24)

I tell you the truth, anyone who has faith in me will do what I have been doing. He will do even greater things than these, because I am going to the Father. And I will do whatever you ask in my name, so that the Son may bring glory to the Father. You may ask me for anything in my name, and I will do it. (John 14:12–14)

If you remain in me and my words remain in you, ask whatever you wish, and it will be given you. (John 15:7)

You did not choose me, but I chose you and appointed you to go and bear fruit—fruit that will last. Then the Father will give you whatever you ask in my name. (John 15:16)

I tell you the truth, my Father will give you whatever you ask in my name. Until now you have not asked for anything in my name. Ask and you will receive, and your joy will be complete. (John 16:23, 24)

Be Specific

The more precise the prayer, the more faith it takes. If you want specific answers to prayer, you need to make specific requests. If you offer only general requests, how will you know if they are answered?

Charles Finney was a skeptical lawyer who was reluctant to become a Christian because none of the Christians he knew received answers to their prayers. Yet after his conversion, he and his associates saw entire towns converted in answer to definite prayers. He said, "Prevailing prayer is specific. It is offered for a definite object. We cannot prevail for everything at once. In all cases recorded in the Bible in which prayer was answered, it is noteworthy that the petitioner prayed for a definite object."[11]

Three Loaves

Jesus taught the value of precise petitions when he told the story of the friend at midnight. Notice that the man did not request "some food." Instead he asked for "three loaves": "Then he said to them, 'Suppose one of you has a friend, and he goes to him at midnight and says, "Friend, lend me *three loaves* of bread . . .""'" (Luke 11:5, emphasis added).

Jesus said the man's boldness in asking specifically, along with his persistence and willingness to come at midnight, would cause his friend to "get up and give him as much as he needs" (Luke 11:8).

Wet Fleece

Gideon believed the Lord had called him to undertake an impossible venture—rescuing Israel from the Midianites. Before he launched into such a bold endeavor, Gideon needed to be sure. So he asked the Lord for definite confirmation.

> Gideon said to God, "If you will save Israel by my hand as you have promised—look, I will place a wool fleece on the threshing floor. If there is dew only on the fleece and all the ground is dry, then I will know that you will save Israel by my hand, as you said." And that is what happened. Gideon rose early the next day; he squeezed the fleece and wrung out the dew—a bowlful of water. (Judges 6:36–38)

Before you get hung up on the legitimacy of putting out a fleece, realize this: Gideon had prayed a very definite prayer and received a definite answer. In essence he had done exactly as Jesus would later instruct, asked for "three loaves," or in this case, "one wet fleece."

Success Today

As we have discussed, Nehemiah was captive in Babylon when he received word that Jerusalem lie in ruin and reproach because her walls had been torn down. Nehemiah longed to rebuild the walls, but he needed permission from the king to leave Babylon and go to Jerusalem. So he asked God to specifically act on the king's heart during their upcoming appointment: "Give your servant success today by granting him favor in the presence of this man" (Nehemiah 1:11).

Nehemiah's request was not without form and void. It was not vague and vapory. No. He gave God a specific target to hit. He asked that God would give him favor that very day as he approached the king about the need in Jerusalem.

Praying for Rain

John R. Rice (1895–1980) was a pastor, an evangelist, and editor of the largest Christian publication of its kind during its time, the *Sword of the Lord* biweekly Christian newspaper. His book *Prayer: Asking and Receiving* is a collection of bold statements, stirring stories, challenging Scriptures, and practical advice about specific prayer. He was adamant in his view that real prayer is asking, and asking for something definite. He said, "Prayer is not only *asking*, but it is *asking something*. It is hardly prayer if it is not definite."[12]

He told of holding a series of evangelistic meetings in a west Texas town in the midst of a terrible drought. Crops and cattle were dying because of the lack of rain.

As he prayed about the drought and the meetings, Rice became convinced God wanted to show his power. So he promised God that as soon as the people were ready to confess their sins and pray for the lost, they would cry out to God to send rain and revival.

When that time came, it was as hot and dry as ever. Yet that night Rice told the people to ask God to send rain within twenty-four hours.

Then Rice boldly announced to the public that they should be prepared for rain in the next twenty-four hours. Only if it came within that time span should they count it as an answer to their prayers.

The next day it was blistering with no hope of rain in the clear sky. The people gathered that morning begging God to show His power by sending rain by the evening service.

Businessmen downtown looked at the sky and scoffed at Rice's bold prediction of rain as a definite answer to prayer. Yet, at two o'clock, for the first time in weeks, a strong wind kicked up and a heavy dark cloud blew in from the southwest. The plate-glass windows of a store where the scoffers had gathered were blown in. The sky ripped open. Rain poured down on the town.

That night the church was packed. That entire town knew God is real and that he answers definite prayers.[13]

Fifty People Saved

About once a year our church had a week of prayer and fasting. One year, the week of prayer and fasting led into a special Bring a Friend Day at church. After praying about it for some time, I felt led to ask our church to pray for fifty adults to be saved the next Sunday on our Bring a Friend Day. Many fasted and prayed for the unsaved and invited them to church.

At that time our church held three Sunday morning worship services. At the end of the first service a couple of people made public confessions of faith in Christ. At the end of the second service nearly a dozen more received Christ. But we had prayed for fifty!

The third service was packed and God was obviously working. I gave the invitation and all over the room, dozens of people gave their lives to Christ. After the service, one of our associate pastors walked up holding a stack of decision cards. He grabbed me and said, "Fifty! Fifty people saved today."

Immediately four men hurried up to me. Eagerly they asked, "How many?"

"How many what?" I teased.

"You know what," they said. "We spent the morning in the prayer chapel asking God to save fifty people in our worship services today."

"You should have prayed for fifty-one."

Those four men, along with many others in our church, had been definite in prayer and God had been definite in answering. God answers definite prayer.

How to Be Definite in Prayer

Let me give several suggestions for becoming more definite, bold, and effective in prayer:

1. Pray about what to pray for. That may sound kind of silly, but what I mean is that it often takes time waiting on God and sorting through our motives to hear his voice clearly so we know what we ought to ask for. I figure that if I'm going to boldly go to the throne of God, I want to be confident about what I'm asking for.
2. Pray about what you really desire. I think it is better to ask for a few definite requests with boldness than to ask for a bunch of things halfheartedly.
3. Search your heart to make sure your motives are pure. Don't ask unless you can ask for something you are certain will glorify God.
4. Go on record. For most things this may mean writing it down. For some requests, it means telling others.

Ask Big

The global ministry of the Navigators was born when twenty-five-year-old Dawson Trotman determined to pray over a map of the world two hours early every morning for forty days. During that season and subsequent years as he poured his life into training men, Dawson Trotman claimed as his own such promises as these:

Call to me and I will answer you and tell you great and unsearchable things you do not know. (Jeremiah 33:3)

Since you are precious and honored in my sight, and because I love you, I will give men in exchange for you, and people in exchange for your life. (Isaiah 43:4)

Your people will rebuild the ancient ruins and will raise up the age-old foundations; you will be called Repairer of Broken Walls, Restorer of Streets with Dwellings. (Isaiah 58:12)

In later years, even as the ministry of the Navigators began to stretch around the world, Trotman often rebuked his colleagues with statements such as "You're not really asking things for the world. Your vision is limited. You need to ask big." If he had to miss a staff meeting, he asked his stand-in to "make a note of what they asked for and tell me. I want to know if they're asking big."[14]

Big Enough to Make the Sun Stand Still

Joshua had the immense challenge of conquering the Promised Land by defeating the pagans. He learned the value of bold faith. One time he asked God for something so large that it is practically beyond imagination. But with an infinite God, nothing is too large to ask. So Joshua asked the Lord to make the sun stand still . . . and God was big enough to do it!

On the day the LORD gave the Amorites over to Israel, Joshua said to the LORD in the presence of Israel: "O sun, stand still over Gibeon, O moon, over the Valley of Aijalon." So the sun stood still, and the moon stopped, till the nation avenged itself on its enemies, as it is written in the Book of Jashar. The sun stopped in the middle of the sky and delayed going down about a full day. There has never been a day like it before or since, a day when the LORD listened to a man. Surely the LORD was fighting for Israel! (Joshua 10:12–14)

Big Enough to Send Fire from Heaven

When I get to heaven, I look forward to meeting Elijah. He was a high-impact spiritual leader who was fearlessly bold when it counted. As you recall, he challenged hundreds of idolatrous pagan priests to a power duel. Both sides would prepare a sacrifice and the God who could answer by fire would be declared the winner and would be worshipped.

The Baal worshippers prayed all day to no avail. Baal was not a prayer-hearing, prayer-answering god.

Elijah raised the stakes by soaking down his sacrifice in water. He knew that no amount of water can dampen the flame of the living God. Then he prayed a big prayer.

> At the time of sacrifice, the prophet Elijah stepped forward and prayed, "O LORD, God of Abraham, Isaac and Israel, let it be known today that you are God in Israel and that I am your servant and have done all these things at your command. Answer me, O LORD, answer me, so these people will know that you, O LORD, are God, and that you are turning their hearts back again." (1 Kings 18:36, 37)

God likes to answer big prayers. They reveal his power and give him glory. They spread his name and prosper his work. They also grow our faith. God answered Elijah's big prayer with an even bigger answer: "Then the fire of the LORD fell and burned up the sacrifice, the wood, the stones and the soil, and also licked up the water in the trench. When all the people saw this, they fell prostrate and cried, 'The LORD—he is God! The LORD—he is God!'" (vv. 38, 39).

Big Enough to Change the Weather

If someone prayed and it impacted the weather for a day, you might be able to consider it a coincidence. But if their prayer affected the weather for three and a half *years*, you would *know* that prayer has power.

Elijah was a man who boldly asked God for big things. The book of James summarizes in a few sentences the story of Elijah's big prayers: "The prayer of a righteous man is powerful and effective. Elijah was a man just like us. He prayed earnestly that it would not rain, and it did not rain on the land for three and a half years. Again he prayed, and the heavens gave rain, and the earth produced its crops" (5:16–18).

Big Enough to Provide a New Car

John R. Rice believed in asking a big God for big things. He wrote, "Ask God for Big Things. He is able!"[15] He also said, "The Bible is a book of marvelous answers to prayer, of big faith, of a bigger God! Never is there a hint anywhere in the Bible that any man ever expected too much from God or that God was ever displeased because one asked for mighty things!"[16]

In 1932 Rice was driving a worn-out old Dodge. He had to push it downhill to get it started. So one Monday he boldly asked God to give him a brand-new car. As he prayed he reminded the Lord that in 1926 he had promised to look after God's business if the Lord would look after his.

On Wednesday Rice got up to speak at his church's midweek service. As he walked to the pulpit one of the men of the church handed him an envelope. Rice was not sure what to think until he noticed the people in the congregation pointing out the window. There was a big, new Chevrolet! Rice looked in the envelope and inside were the keys, title, and warranty to that new Chevy.

The men of the church had raised money to get Rice a new car. He did not know of their plans. But God did. They did not know of Rice's bold prayer. But God did.

Big Enough to Pay the Bills

In 1936 Rice was called to preside over a ten-day meeting in a far-away city. After arriving, he was crushed to find that no money had been spent to advertise the meetings and that the crowd was tiny, not more than fifty people. The church was strapped financially and the offering of $25 barely covered his travel expenses. On top of that, he desperately needed $920 (a large amount of money in the Depression year of 1936) to cover the cost of printing and mailing his popular evangelistic newspaper, the *Sword of the Lord*. Rice had counted on the offerings from this ten-day meeting to cover the expenses for mailing his newspaper.

Rice wrote that with tears in his eyes, he boldly told the Lord that the bills were his (God's) problem because they were incurred doing his work: "It is your paper, not mine. I did not save myself; I did not call myself to preach. If you want a paper You must pay the bills . . . Lord, it is up to you to pay those bills."[17]

The next morning on the train home, the porter came through the car holding a telegram and calling Rice's name. Rice took the telegram. It was from his secretary and it simply said:

YOU HAVE JUST RECEIVED A CHECK FOR ONE THOUSAND DOLLARS FOR YOUR WORK!

The money was from a man Rice had never seen, never written to, nor communicated with in any other way![18] But we all know that, ultimately, the large amount of money did not come from man. It came from God, the God who is big enough to answer big, bold, specific prayers.

APPLICATION WORKSHEET

What are two or three key thoughts you want to remember from this chapter?

1.

2.

3.

What are the big things in your life and ministry only God can do?

How do you plan to apply these aspects of bold prayer to those needs?

Claim God's Promises:

Be specific:

Ask big:

CHAPTER 8

Build on the Basics

. . . but I am a man of prayer. (Psalm 109:4)

RECENTLY, I was rereading the psalms of David. As I did, I was pondering the true secret of David's greatness as a leader and stumbled onto a phrase that jumped out at me as if it were written in bold print, or better, as if it were spray painted in neon. David penned Psalm 109 as he faced persecution. In verses 2–4, after describing the fierce opposition he was facing, at the end of verse 4 David simply wrote, ". . . but I am a man of prayer."

In the Hebrew, this multiword phrase is all one word, *tĕphillah*, meaning "prayer." It could describe "an intercession, a supplication, or song." Some translate this word in its context as "I give myself to prayer" (KJV and ESV), or "But I resort to prayer" (Amplified Bible), or "But I am in prayer" (NASB). I prefer Spurgeon's view that David is saying in response to the persecution, "I became prayer."[1]

I especially like the way Adolph Saphir renders this word *tĕphillah* in Psalm 109, as simply, "I prayer" or "I'm prayer."[2] Prayer was such a part of David's life that it defined him. His life was prayer. I love it!

What was David's secret? What made him a man whose heart beat in rhythm with God's (Acts 13:22)? Why was David a man God trusted to shepherd God's people? One phrase says it all: ". . . but I am a man of prayer." Better yet, one word says it all: "prayer."

A Balanced Variety of Prayers

David was shepherd, musician, giant killer, soldier, fugitive, Robin Hood figure, military general, king, songwriter, and worship leader. He was an incredible leader. But make no mistake—every good thing he accomplished flowed from the fact he was a man of prayer.

With most Bible characters and great leaders from church history we have record of just a few of their prayers. But with David we have a whole book full of his prayers. They were penned during the most significant and extreme times in his life. Few men have experienced loftier highs or deeper lows. What is significant for us to note is that in all occasions and locations, mountaintop or valley, David prayed.

Not only did David pray, but he prayed a variety of prayers. David prayed simple prayers and complex ones. He prayed tears. He asked questions. He made bold resolutions and prayed big prayers of faith. He also used balance. He prayed prayers of adoration, confession, thanksgiving, and supplication.

God is a person. He has personality. We are people. We have personality. Prayer is expressing the many facets of our personality and our situation to the many aspects of God's personality. One type of prayer will not do. We need to pray with all kinds of prayers (Ephesians 6:18).

As I have studied the prayer lives of dozens of high-impact spiritual leaders, I notice that as with David, prayer was a defining characteristic of their lives. I have also noticed that as did David, they used both a diversity of prayers and a balance of the primary types of prayer.

The Model Prayer

Jesus taught his followers to pray with both balance and variety. Notice the elements of praise, petition, and confession as you think through his model prayer:

> This, then, is how you should pray: "Our Father in heaven, hallowed be your name, your kingdom come, your will be done on earth as it is in heaven. Give us today our daily bread. Forgive us our debts, as we also have forgiven our debtors. And lead us not into temptation, but deliver us from the evil one." (Matthew 6:9–13)

Dr. Elmer Towns studied the largest churches in the world. One of his unexpected discoveries was that many of the pastors of the world's biggest congregations frequently prayed through the model, or Lord's Prayer, outline. One of the pastors stated, "Each day I pray the rounds. Like a runner who jogs around and around a race track to get physically fit, I pray the rounds several times each day . . . To pray the rounds is to pray the Lord's Prayer several times a day."[3]

The A.C.T.S. of Prayer . . . Rearranged

I try to pray through the Lord's Prayer at least once a day. I like the balanced nature of it, including praise, petition, and confession. I also appreciate the way the first few lines ("your name, your kingdom, your will") readjust my priorities.

As a young follower of Jesus, I learned an acrostic that also helped me bring variety and balance to my prayers. This acrostic contains the major elements given by Christ in the model prayer. You might be familiar with it: ACTS.

A: Adoration
C: Confession
T: Thanksgiving
S: Supplication

Using each letter as a heading, you can pray through this acrostic in a matter of minutes or stretch it over hours. I can do it in four or five sentences, or I have spent as much as an hour on each section.

I usually change the order (T.A.C.S.), putting Thanksgiving first, followed by Adoration. That way I can follow the prescription of Psalm 100:4, which says, "Enter his gates *with thanksgiving* and his courts *with praise*; give thanks to him and praise his name" (emphasis added).

A study of the prayers of David and the lives of high-impact spiritual leaders reveals that they also used these same primary types of prayers. As you study these basic forms of prayer, be challenged to stay out of a rut and deepen your relationship with our infinite God through a balanced assortment of daily prayers.

T: THANKSGIVING

David loved God and knew the glorious power of his presence. Nothing brought him greater joy than the opportunity to bless his people by returning to Israel the ark of the covenant, the wooden box that symbolized the manifest presence of God. As a result, he intentionally prioritized thanksgiving into the daily life of Israel.

On the day the ark was brought home to Jerusalem, David assigned some Levites to make a permanent practice to give thanks to the Lord. He even wrote a prayer of thanks for them to sing.

> Give thanks to the LORD, call on his name; make known among the nations what he has done . . . Give thanks to the LORD, for he is good; his love endures forever. Cry out, "Save us, O God

our Savior; gather us and deliver us from the nations, that we may give thanks to your holy name, that we may glory in your praise." (1 Chronicles 16:8, 34, 35)

David repeated his theme "Give thanks to the LORD, for he is good; his love endures forever" in many of his psalms (106:1; 107:1; 136:1). In fact, an argument could be made that "Give thanks to the LORD, for he is good; his love endures forever" was the most used hymn in the Bible. It was the "Amazing Grace," "How Great Thou Art," and "Shout to the Lord" of the people of God for centuries.

For example, when Solomon had finished the temple and was bringing the ark to reside there, he instructed all the Levites to dress in fine linen and to play cymbals, harps, and lyres. In addition, 120 more priests were to accompany them sounding trumpets. Then the musicians and singers were to join in unison to give thanks to the Lord. The song they sang?

He is good; his love endures forever. (2 Chronicles 5:13)

Give Thanks to the Lord (part 2)

When Solomon finished building the temple, a special service of dedication was held. God was pleased and expressed it, as fire came down from heaven and consumed the burnt offering and the sacrifices. The glory of the Lord filled the temple. It must have been an amazing sight, as the glory of the Lord was so thick, the priests could not even enter the temple of the Lord!

Then the massive crowd of Israelites who had seen the fire coming down and the glory of the Lord above the temple responded with thanks. They knelt on the pavement with their faces to the ground. Then they worshipped, giving thanks to the Lord. Guess what they sang!

He is good; his love endures forever. (2 Chronicles 7:4)

Give Thanks to the Lord (part 3)

Years after Solomon, Judah's King Jehoshaphat faced a fearsome threat from three armies. Wisely he called the nation to fast and pray for deliverance. When God promised to fight for them, Jehoshaphat came up with one of the most bizarre battle plans in history. It was based entirely on faith and thanksgiving. Read it for yourself:

> After consulting the people, Jehoshaphat appointed men to sing to the LORD and to praise him for the splendor of his holiness as they went out at the head of the army, saying: "Give thanks to the LORD, for his love endures forever." (2 Chronicles 20:21)

I would love to have heard the discussion among the men who led the army into battle without shields, swords, or chariots. Their only weapon was thanksgiving. Humanly speaking, it would have been suicide. But this battle belonged to the Lord. Fortunately, thanksgiving was more than enough. Read what happened:

> As they began to sing and praise, the LORD set ambushes against the men of Ammon and Moab and Mount Seir who were invading Judah, and they were defeated. The men of Ammon and Moab rose up against the men from Mount Seir to destroy and annihilate them. After they finished slaughtering the men from Seir, they helped to destroy one another.
>
> When the men of Judah came to the place that overlooks the desert and looked toward the vast army, they saw only dead bodies lying on the ground; no one had escaped. So Jehoshaphat and his men went to carry off their plunder, and they found among them a great amount of equipment and clothing and also articles of value—more than they could take away. There was so much plunder that it took three days to collect it. . . . The fear of God came upon all the kingdoms of the countries when they heard how the LORD had fought against

the enemies of Israel. And the kingdom of Jehoshaphat was at peace, for his God had given him rest on every side. (2 Chronicles 20:22–25, 29, 30)

Give Thanks to the Lord (part 4)

The Jews had been living in exile in Babylon for seventy years. Just as the Lord had predicted, King Cyrus decreed that they could begin to return to their homeland. Their first task was to rebuild the temple. They were awed by the privilege and responsibility of restoring temple worship to Jerusalem. When they laid the foundation, there was only one song that fulfilled the prophecy and fit the occasion:

> Give thanks to the LORD Almighty, for the LORD is good; his love endures forever. (Jeremiah 33:11; see also Ezra 3:10, 11)

The Nature of Thanksgiving

Thanksgiving is verbalizing the attitude of gratitude. It is expressing appreciation to God for his generosity. It is saying "Thank you" for the specific gifts he has given you. It is an indication of humility and the cure for complaining.

The Habit of Thanksgiving in the Shadow of the Lion's Den

King Darius was the new ruler of the Medes and Persians. As Darius was appointing a new cabinet, Daniel's political rivals wanted to cut Daniel out of power. Yet Daniel had no skeletons in his closet.

They knew prayer was such a part of Daniel's leadership life that he would not cease his thrice-daily prayers. So they hatched a scheme to trick the king into making a law that, for the next thirty days, anyone praying to any man or god other than the king would be thrown to the lions. Darius ignorantly signed it.

I want you to carefully note Daniel's response: "Now when Daniel learned that the decree had been published, he went home to his upstairs room where the windows opened toward Jerusalem. Three times a day he got down on his knees and prayed, giving thanks to his God, just as he had done before" (Daniel 6:10).

Notice that last phrase—*"giving thanks to his God, just as he had done before."* Daniel was an outstanding leader who eventually served as prime minister in one of the largest empires in history. He made thanksgiving the essential element of his prayers. Even when it was tough, Daniel practiced gratitude. It was a holy habit in his life. He gave thanks *just as he always had.*

As you know, Daniel was not spared *from* the lions' den. But God responded to his habit of gratitude and went *with* him into the lions' den. As a result, he came out unharmed. On top of that, seeing Daniel spared, Darius executed Daniel's enemies. Beyond that, Darius issued a new decree that the people of his kingdom were to reverence the God of Daniel!

Thanks for Fleas

Corrie ten Boom (1892–1983) was a Dutch Christian who helped many Jews escape the Nazis during World War II. Because of her efforts she was sent to the notorious Ravensbruck concentration camp in Germany. Her sister and her father died in the concentration camps, but miraculously she survived. She left the camp as a very effective spiritual leader who returned to Holland and set up rehabilitation centers for Germans who worked under the Nazi regime.

While in the concentration camp, Corrie learned the power of thanksgiving prayers. Her sister, Betsy, challenged her to give thanks in *all* circumstances, including giving thanks for the fleas that infested their crude, cold, wooden dormitory. Corrie struggled to do so.

A few weeks later, the ten Boom sisters had attracted a crowd of prisoners each night as they read the Bible under a lightbulb. Corrie was shocked that no guard disturbed this nightly Bible study. One night Corrie asked a woman, "Why don't the guards ever come into the dormitory?"

The woman answered, "They are repelled by the fleas."[4]

"I thank my God for you."

Paul was an amazing leader who lived the life of prayer. Often, he was called to lead people like the Corinthians, who were difficult to lead and even rejected his authority. Yet he also displayed a remarkable ability to avoid bitterness and maintain an open heart toward them. How was this possible? Paul believed in the power of thanksgiving. "I always thank God for you because of his grace given you in Christ Jesus" (1 Corinthians 1:4).

No matter whom he was praying for, Paul made it a practice to fill each intercession with gratitude. Note the familiar note of thanksgiving seasoning his letters:

> First, I thank my God through Jesus Christ for all of you, because your faith is being reported all over the world. (Romans 1:8)

> I have not stopped giving thanks for you, remembering you in my prayers. (Ephesians 1:16)

> I thank my God every time I remember you. (Philippians 1:3)

> We always thank God, the Father of our Lord Jesus Christ, when we pray for you. (Colossians 1:3)

> We always thank God for all of you, mentioning you in our prayers. (1 Thessalonians 1:2)

> We ought always to thank God for you, brothers. (2 Thessalonians 1:3)

> I thank God, whom I serve . . . as night and day I constantly remember you in my prayers. (2 Timothy 1:3)

> I always thank my God as I remember you in my prayers. (Philemon 1:4)

In fact, Paul even encouraged the young leader Timothy to follow his example of seasoning every intercession with thanksgiving: "I urge, then, first of all, that requests, prayers, intercession and thanksgiving be made for everyone" (1 Timothy 2:1).

Start the Day with Thanksgiving

Jerry Falwell was an entrepreneurial spiritual leader. His church grew to more than twenty thousand members. He started and led what has become the largest evangelical university in history. He believed that "[p]rayer is the center of the Christian life."[5] Even though he was an advocate of many types of prayer, he was especially fond of thanksgiving, stating,

> Often the best and most productive kind of praying is the prayer of thanksgiving. For these thirty-five years I have begun each day with prayers of thanks to God for Who He is and for all He is doing in my life and the lives of my family, my friends, and my church. You cannot imagine how the shape of your day can be changed when you begin with prayers of thanks . . . See how grateful you can be. Add to your gratitude list every possible good thing in your life at this time and in the past. Look ahead and thank Him for the blessings yet to come. Fill your life with thanksgiving. Develop the attitude of gratitude. Even if you don't feel particularly grateful at that moment, thank Him!

The very act of praying prayers of thanksgiving can transform a black and ugly day into a day of joy and wonderful surprises.[6]

Applying Thanksgiving

Make Your Own Thanksgiving List

See if you can list fifty things for which you are grateful. Begin with spiritual blessings like the Bible, answered prayer, heaven, forgiveness, the Holy Spirit, and your church. Try to list at least ten spiritual blessings.

Now list some physical blessings such as the ability to see, walk, taste, and smell. Thank God for your material blessings, such as a place to live, clothes, food, a car, furniture, books, and so forth. Say "Thanks" to God for meeting various financial needs.

Thank God for lessons he has been teaching you lately. Also thank him regarding trials he has seen you through and how they have benefited your life. Thank God for things you believe he is going to do for you in the future.

Say "Thanks" to God for key people in your life. Think of family and friends, fellow workers, and neighbors. Thank God for authorities and spiritual mentors. Conclude by giving thanks for pastors, teachers, and missionaries you know.

Cultivate an Attitude of Gratitude

For the next twenty-four hours, or longer, make a conscious attempt to make certain that the only prayers you pray are "saying thanks" prayers. Turn every prayer into an expression of gratitude.

Be Thankful Every Hour

For the next few days, every time you notice the hour changing, say "Thanks" to God for something. I had a friend who went so far as to set the alarm on his watch to go off every hour to remind him to give thanks. He reported that within a week, it had wonderfully changed his attitude and walk with God.

Give God a Minute of Thanks

God gives us 1,440 minutes each day. I encourage you to pause for the next minute and see if you can think of five things to thank God for.

A: ADORATION (PRAISE)

Praise is essentially a positive response to who God is. Jesus taught us to begin our prayers with praise when he said, "This, then, is how you should pray: 'Our Father in heaven, hallowed be your name'" (Matthew 6:9). Nehemiah opened his prayer with praise, referring to the Lord as "the great and awesome God, who keeps his covenant of love with those who love him and obey his commands" (Nehemiah 1:5).

Praise and thanksgiving are always good places to begin when we pray. By beginning with God, we are stating our priorities and putting our and others' needs into perspective.

I think many of us are drawn to David because he lived life with a wide-open, authentic, sincere relationship with God. Just as he was diligent to cry out to God with bold honesty, he was just as diligent to humbly give God praise. Adoration, or praise, dominates the prayers of David. He is the ultimate worship leader. He played, sang, wrote, and danced praise to the Lord.

More than a hundred times David uses the word *praise* in his prayers recorded in the Psalms. The Hebrew word *Psalms*, in fact, is the word for "praises" (*tēhillah*). David's life of praise was so rich that he used many different Hebrew words to describe the full-orbed praises that saturate his prayers.

1. *Yadah*, meaning "to thank or praise" (Psalm 9:1)
2. *Zamar*, used to mean "to sing praise, to make music; to play a musical instrument" (Psalm 9:2, 11)
3. *Tĕhillah*, which means "to give public praise; song or hymn of praise" (Psalm 22:3, 25)
4. *Halal* was one of David's favorite terms for praise. It means "to celebrate or to boast." It is the same term from which we get our word *Hallelujah*, which means "praise the Lord" (Psalm 22:22; 34:2).
5. *Barak* was also quite popular with David. It means "to kneel or to bless" (Psalm 34:1).
6. *Todah* means "confession, praise, and thanksgiving." It could describe "a song or a thank offering" (Psalm 69:30).
7. *Shabach* is only used a few times by David. It means "to laud, praise, commend" (Psalm 63:3, 4; 145:4).
8. *Ranan* is a word that describes a way to offer praise. It means "to cry out, shout, or sing for joy; to give a ringing cry" (Psalm 5:11).

Singing Praise

Of course David was not the only spiritual leader to value and practice praise. Since the time of David, if not earlier, it has been the practice of spiritual leaders to sing prayers of praise. The hymnbook is sprinkled with such prayers. You can tell them because they end with the word *amen*. Many of the recent praise-and-worship songs are prayers.

Augustine was a philosopher and theologian and served as bishop of the North African city of Hippo. Augustine (354–430) was one of the most important figures in the development of Western Christianity. What I find personally challenging is that such a noted theologian had such a deep appreciation and understanding of praise. He wrote, "To sing once is to pray twice."[7]

Another towering spiritual leader, Martin Luther, was also a strong practitioner of praise. He penned the words of the great hymn, "A Mighty Fortress Is Our God." Highly practical, he said, "When I cannot pray, I always sing."[8]

The Power of Prison Praise

Paul and Silas were among the first missionaries in the early church. Soon after they arrived in Philippi hoping to plant a church, they found themselves in prison. They had cast a demon out of a fortune-telling slave girl. However, the girl's owners did not appreciate the loss of potential income, so they stirred up the crowd and the authorities against Paul and Silas. As a result, the missionaries were severely beaten and taken to the inner cell of the prison, where their feet were locked in stocks.

I don't know what you would do, but I have a tendency toward self-pity. Such a rotten time would lead me to pout and whine—but not Paul and Silas. They refused the urge to pout and whine, and instead they embraced praise and worship. The Bible says it this way: "About midnight Paul and Silas were praying and singing hymns to God" (Acts 16:25). For them, praise was powerful. When they started praising, God started working.

> Suddenly there was such a violent earthquake that the foundations of the prison were shaken. At once all the prison doors flew open, and everybody's chains came loose. The jailer woke up, and when he saw the prison doors open, he drew his sword and was about to kill himself because he thought the prisoners had escaped. But Paul shouted, "Don't harm yourself! We are all here!"
>
> The jailer called for lights, rushed in and fell trembling before Paul and Silas. He then brought them out and asked, "Sirs, what must I do to be saved?" (Acts 16:26–30)

Praise the Lord Anyway

Habakkuk was a spiritual leader who struggled against the sovereignty of God. His heart broken by the sin, strife, and oppression that dragged Judah down, Habakkuk cried out to God, but God seemingly did nothing. Listen to the frustration in his prayer: "How long, O LORD, must I call for help, but you do not listen?" (Habakkuk 1:2).

When God did answer, the response was not what Habakkuk wanted. The Lord told him he planned to use the ruthless Babylonians to bring judgment. In an act of faith and submission to the will and ways of sovereign God, Habakkuk responded with a tremendous outburst of praise. His song is recorded in the entire third chapter of the book bearing his name. Note the powerful praise at the beginning and the end:

> LORD, I have heard of your fame; I stand in awe of your deeds, O LORD. Renew them in our day, in our time make them known; in wrath remember mercy . . . yet I will rejoice in the LORD, I will be joyful in God my Savior. The Sovereign LORD is my strength; he makes my feet like the feet of a deer, he enables me to go on the heights. (Habakkuk 3:2, 19)

Praise to the Very End

John and Charles Wesley helped catalyze the Great Awakening and fathered the Methodist Church. They also lived a life of praise.

Charles (1707–1788) was one of the greatest songwriters in history. He wrote such enduring classics of praise as "And Can It Be That I Should Gain?," "Hark the Herald Angels Sing," and "O for a Thousand Tongues to Sing." Because of his songs, the Methodist movement was a movement fueled on the wings of praise.

Fittingly, some of his brother John's last words on this earth were spoken as he sang a hymn:

> *I'll praise my Maker while I've breath,*
> *And when my voice is lost in death,*
> *Praise shall employ my nobler pow'rs;*
> *My days of praise shall ne'er be past,*
> *While life, and thought, and being last,*
> *Or immortality endures.*

Soon after, as John Wesley was slipping from this life into the next, he requested that those gathered around his bed fill the air with prayer and praise. His very last words were "I'll praise—I'll praise!"[9]

Applying Praise

1. Open every prayer with a sentence or two of praise. Hallow God's name.
2. Listen to and sing along with praise music in your car, home, and workplace.
3. When in a corporate worship gathering, actively enter into praise. Don't let your mind be filled with a thousand other details. Concentrate on the words. More importantly, picture the One they were written for and sing them as if you are in the throne room of the King of kings, because in a very real sense, you will be.

Confession

It was ugly. In his midlife season King David had a crisis. Bored and weary, he opted out of responsibility (2 Samuel 11:1). With his defenses down, he foolishly initiated an illicit sexual encounter with a married woman named Bathsheba. She became pregnant (vv. 2–5). Desperately he tried to hide his sin under a blanket of deception. It failed, because ironically Bathsheba's husband, Uriah, displayed the character and commitment David lacked (vv. 6–13). Frantically and decisively, David blatantly misused his power to have Uriah killed in battle (vv. 14–27). He then married Bathsheba, assuming "no one would ever know."

But David knew . . . and, of course, God knew. God always knows.

Guilt is horrible, hideous, terrible, and terrifying. Yet God is merciful. He does not abandon us to be swallowed in the sickening cesspool of our guilt. Instead, he pursues us. His Spirit haunts us. His Word hunts us down and speaks to us.

God's love, Spirit, and words of rebuke chased David down. The messenger was the prophet Nathan. Nathan skillfully rebuked David and cut him straight through the heart with four chilling words: "You are the man" (2 Samuel 12:1, 7–9).

David knew exactly what Nathan meant. David was caught. He could hide no longer and he knew it. Immediately he said the only words that can erase the awful stains of guilt: "I have sinned against the Lord" (2 Samuel 12:13).

After David admitted his sin, God's grace and mercy were spilled out on his behalf. Nathan spoke the best words a guilty soul can ever hear: "The Lord has taken away your sin" (2 Samuel 12:13).

Later David recorded his experience in a powerful psalm:

> Have mercy on me, O God, according to your unfailing love; according to your great compassion blot out my transgressions. Wash away all my iniquity and cleanse me from my sin . . .
>
> Cleanse me with hyssop, and I will be clean; wash me, and I will be whiter than snow. Let me hear joy and gladness; let the bones you have crushed rejoice. Hide your face from my sins and blot out all my iniquity.
>
> Create in me a pure heart, O God, and renew a steadfast spirit within me. Do not cast me from your presence or take

your Holy Spirit from me. Restore to me the joy of your salvation and grant me a willing spirit, to sustain me.

Then I will teach transgressors your ways, and sinners will turn back to you. Save me from bloodguilt, O God, the God who saves me, and my tongue will sing of your righteousness.

O LORD, open my lips, and my mouth will declare your praise.

You do not delight in sacrifice, or I would bring it; you do not take pleasure in burnt offerings. The sacrifices of God are a broken spirit; a broken and contrite heart, O God, you will not despise. (Psalm 51:1, 2, 7–17)

Leaders sin . . . even great ones. The wise ones confess their sins.

"I confess."

Before Nehemiah began his great undertaking for the Lord, he confessed sin. He accepted responsibility and owned up to his sin, the sin of his father's house, and the sins of his people: "I confess the sins we Israelites, including myself and my father's house, have committed against you. We have acted very wickedly toward you. We have not obeyed the commands, decrees and laws you gave your servant Moses" (Nehemiah 1:6, 7).

Maybe God has laid something big and important on *your* heart. Before diving in, make sure you are cleansed of sin.

"Woe is me!"

Isaiah had an incredible experience of being ushered into the throne room of God. He described the Lord as exalted above all. Beyond that, he saw the Lord surrounded by the amazing seraphim, the unique angels who perpetually blaze in the presence of the holy Lord God. They not only blaze perpetually, but they also continually cry out in harmonious epiphany the one attribute of God that stands out above the rest—holiness—absolute separation from any and all sin. Such a sight floored Isaiah and exposed his sin and the sin of his people. His only response was to declare his guilt and confess the sin.

> I saw the LORD seated on a throne, high and exalted, and the train of his robe filled the temple. Above him were seraphs, each with six wings: With two wings they covered their faces, with two they covered their feet, and with two they were flying. And they were calling to one another:
> "Holy, holy, holy is the LORD Almighty; the whole earth is full of his glory . . ."
> "Woe to me!" I cried. "I am ruined! For I am a man of unclean lips, and I live among a people of unclean lips, and my eyes have seen the King, the LORD Almighty." (Isaiah 6:1–3, 5)

In the next few verses we read that Isaiah received his calling as a prophet and began his ministry. But remember—he dealt decisively with sin first. God does not use dirty vessels. We must be clean if we hope to be used.

The Nature of Confession

Confessing sin is agreeing with God about the existence and seriousness of our sin. It is letting the sin in our hearts break our hearts. It is seeing sin as God sees it. It is allowing the pain our sin caused the Father and Jesus on the cross to fill our thoughts, stir our emotions, and change our wills. It is saying the same thing about our sins that God says.

It is not enough to let the Lord examine our hearts and show us our sin. We must take the next step and let our sorrow over that sin lead us to confess it—not excuse it, rationalize it, or blame it on someone else, but confess it.

"If we confess our sins . . ."

The apostle John strongly believed that the ongoing confession of sin was necessary for an ongoing intimate relationship with God. He also reminded us of God's willingness to forgive our sin:

> This is the message we have heard from him and declare to you: God is light; in him there is no darkness at all. If we claim to have fellowship with him yet walk in the darkness, we lie and do not live by the truth. But if we walk in the light, as he is in the light, we have fellowship with one another, and the blood of Jesus, his Son, purifies us from all sin. If we claim to be without sin, we deceive ourselves and the truth is not in us. If we confess our sins, he is faithful and just and will forgive us our sins and purify us from all unrighteousness. (1 John 1:5–9)

Applying Confession

1. While we count it important to wash our physical bodies every day, it is even more important to make certain our souls are cleansed on a daily basis as well. Spiritual cleansing comes from washing in the Word *and* confessing sin. If you don't already, take some time each day to look back through your life and confess every sin.

2. Just as a house may be cleaned weekly, it also needs a thorough cleaning once or twice a year. Plan an hour or so every few months to sit in the presence of God and ask him to reveal any sin. Notice that these times are kind of like peeling an onion. There are layers. First, God addresses the obvious outward sins. Then he often peels into the deeper sins of heart and attitude.

Supplication

Supplication is simply asking God to *supply* needs. Supplication can be offered for your own needs or for the needs of others. It is praying "Give us this day our daily bread." It is spreading your problems out before the Lord and letting him sort them out. It is replacing worry with prayer. It is turning every pressure and problem into prayer. It is making your worry list into your prayer list. It is refusing to worry because you are choosing to pray. It is casting all your cares on him because he cares for you.

John Bunyan's (1628–1688) book *Pilgrim's Progress* is second only to the Bible as the most popular book in history. Bunyan wrote most of that book while suffering in prison for preaching the gospel. He understood the Christian life as few men ever have. He also understood prayer. Writing from prison in 1662 he gave a textbook definition of prayer as supplication: "Prayer is a sincere, sensible, affectionate pouring out of the heart or soul to God, through Christ, in the strength and assistance of the Holy Spirit, for such things as God hath promised, or according to the Word, for the good of the church, with submission, in faith, to the will of God."[10]

"Give us today our daily bread."

Jesus taught his disciples to ask God for their daily needs (Matthew 6:11). The Lord has shown himself faithful to meet the needs of his people.

God gave the children of Israel manna from heaven for forty years, six miracles a week, year in and year out (Exodus 16:35). He kept their garments and shoes from wearing out for forty years (Deuteronomy 29:5). The Lord gave them quail when they wanted meat (Exodus 16:13; Numbers 11:31). He gave them water when they were thirsty (Numbers 20:11).

God used ravens to feed Elijah (1 Kings 17:3–6). He fed Elijah, a widow, and her son for days with just a handful of meal and a bit of oil (vv. 9–16). Later, he sent an angel to bake Elijah a cake and to give him some water (1 Kings 19:5–7).

Jesus led his disciples to catch so many fish their nets began to break (Luke 5:4–8). Once he fed five thousand men and their families with a boy's lunch (Luke 9:10–17). Later he fed four thousand men and their families with an equally tiny amount (Matthew 15:29–38).

The God who did all this back then is vitally interested in *your* prayers now. He has not changed. He is still willing and able to provide *your* daily needs. You need to ask.

Prayer: Asking and Receiving

John R. Rice was a pastor, evangelist, and the editor of a once highly influential biweekly Christian newspaper called the *Sword of the Lord*, which had a circulation of more than ninety thousand. His books and pamphlets totaled more than sixty million copies in print.

He was a simple man with a simple view of prayer and its power. He understood the nature and power of supplication when he said, "Prayer is asking something definite from God."[11] He further stated, "Remember prayer is ASKING. Remember the answer to prayer is HAVING."[12]

Daily Provisions

Dawson Trotman, the founder of the Navigators, and his young wife Lila freely gave themselves to disciple sailors. He quit his job to minister full-time by opening up their home so they could house sailors for a few days at a time and he would be free to disciple them. Regularly the needs surpassed the couple's tiny income. Supplication, asking God to supply "daily bread," was an everyday element of their lives. His biographer wrote:

> Expenses soon mounted above income . . . the prayer for daily bread was still a daily matter, as an incident typical of those early days shows. With an apartment full of sailors, some sleeping on the floor, Daws and Lila had gone to their room and prayed

before retiring, including a request for food for the morning. After midnight a knock on their door brought [a] sailor who handed Daws a dollar . . . Waiting until all hands were asleep, Daws slipped out . . . and went shopping. At an all-night market he bought enough bacon, eggs, bread, and margarine for breakfast for the unsuspecting group.[13]

Later his biographer wrote:

For nearly four years of Navigators ministry Daws and Lila held to the practice of not mentioning financial needs and trusting God to provide. Without self-pity, in a spirit of expectancy they marveled at the ways He did it. So regular was His supply that even critical victories were recorded as routine. A check came in time to cover the utilities bill. A serviceman handed him money that bought gasoline, groceries, and postage stamps. . . . The driver of a milk truck, which had broken down, knocked on their door asking if they could use a large quantity of milk that would have spoiled.[14]

Daily Provisions (part 2)

Possibly no leader was better at maintaining a daily conversation with the Lord about his daily need and the needs of his ministry than George Müller. Müller is the man who established and built 117 schools that educated more than 120,000 young persons. He saw the provision of every article of clothing and every meal for more than ten thousand orphans every day by faith and prayer only, without ever taking a public collection or ever appealing to any man for money.

Müller's consistent faith in prayer is astounding. He stated that over the course of his life he saw more than fifty thousand answers to his petitions! Beyond that, he also declared that thirty thousand of those came *in the same day (or hour)* in which they were asked for![15] Every day he asked the Lord to supply needs. Every day the Lord did.

Applying Supplication

1. Make a list of the top ten personal needs in your life. Pray for these at least once a day.
2. List the top ten needs in your current ministry. Pray for these once a day yourself and at least weekly with the others involved with you in ministry.
3. Create several separate short lists of requests. Make one for your family members. Make one for lost people. Make one for missionaries. Make one for the leaders serving over you and also one for the leaders serving under you. Pray for these *at least* once a week.

APPLICATION WORKSHEET

What are two or three key thoughts you want to remember from this chapter?

1.

2.

3.

How will you apply the following?

Thanksgiving:

Adoration:

Confession:

Supplication:

CHAPTER 9

Adopt Best Practices

As I STUDIED the lives of high-impact leaders, I noticed there were some prayer practices not necessarily used by all of them, but certainly worth learning. In many ways they were some of the best practices of some of the best leaders and prayer warriors. In this chapter we will briefly study these best practices. I'm certain you can find a few that will aid and enhance your prayer life.

Pray without Ceasing—Paul and Spurgeon

Paul was one of the greatest spiritual leaders to ever walk the earth. From planting churches to writing what is now a large chunk of our New Testament, he made a difference. His success, in part, certainly flowed from his prayer life. His letters are sprinkled with examples and teachings about prayer. One of the commands he gave that most of us know is the miniature, yet mighty, command "Pray continually" (1 Thessalonians 5:17). These two words are easy to say but much harder to apply.

Charles Spurgeon, the successful English pastor who preached to crowds of ten thousand every Sunday, was one leader who both understood and mastered Paul's injunction. When he preached on this passage, he explained:

> While your hands are busy with the world, let your hearts still talk with God; not in twenty sentences at a time, for such an interval might be inconsistent with your calling, but in broken sentences and interjections . . . or, without words we may pray in the upward glancing of the eye or the sigh of the heart. He who prays without ceasing uses many little darts and hand-grenades of godly desire, which he casts forth at every available interval. Sometimes he will blow the furnace of his desires to a great heat in regular prayer, and as a consequence at other times, the sparks will continue to rise up to heaven in the form of brief words, and looks, and desires.[1]

Spurgeon's biographer observed, "If we may venture to observe the inner life of this man so greatly honored of God in the world, we shall not find Spurgeon on his knees; and that not because he did not pray but because he prayed incessantly."[2] Spurgeon's simple explanation was "I always feel it well just to put a few words of prayer between everything I do."[3]

One of his friends recounted walking down a road near a wood when Spurgeon casually paused and invited the friend to join him on his knees. There Spurgeon "lifted his soul to God in the most loving and yet, reverent prayer . . . It was something that belonged as much to the habit of his mind as breathing did to the habit of his body."[4]

Applying Unceasing Prayer

1. Try to pray a sentence or two before every new activity you perform today.
2. Try to turn every conscious thought back to the Lord in a simple one- or two-word prayer, such as "Thanks," "Help," or "Bless."

Persevering Petitions—George Müller

As we have mentioned previously, George Müller was one of the most effective spiritual leaders the world has ever seen. Gifted as a philanthropist, evangelist, and pastor, God used him to accomplish amazing things. He circulated 111 million Bible tracts and pamphlets, 1.4 million New Testaments, and 275,000 Bibles in different languages, with nearly as many smaller portions of Scripture. He supported 189 missionaries. After he turned seventy, he preached the gospel in forty-two nations to approximately three million people. During his life, he cared for more than 10,000 orphans, provided education for 123,000 students, and received $7,500,000 of unsolicited funds from a multitude of human sources by faith and prayer alone.

His unique financial policy was to ask no one but God to meet his needs and the needs of his ever-expanding ministry. He clearly stated the major goal of his orphanages: "The primary object of the work is to show the whole world . . . that even in these last evil days the living God is ready to prove Himself as the living God, being ever willing to help . . . and answer the prayers of those who trust in Him."[5]

One of the aspects of Müller's remarkable prayer life was his practice of persisting in petitioning God *until* the answer was given. The man stubbornly refused to quit.

On occasions when hope seemed lost and answers slow in coming, he simply increased the frequency and number of his petitions. For example, when they desperately needed additional workers, Müller had his existing staff triple their daily prayer times: "Instead of praying once a day about this matter, as we had been doing day after day for years, we met daily three times, to bring this before God."[6]

When he needed a huge amount of money to expand his orphan ministry with two new, large orphans' houses, Müller multiplied his requests and hammered heaven for the needed money.

During this time he wrote, "Many and great may be the difficulties. Thousands and thousands of prayers may have to ascend to God before the full answer is obtained."[7]

He did his part by offering thousands of prayers over the span of several years, and God responded. Steadily money poured in from all over the world. When the last of the donations arrived Müller gave thanks, saying, "Thousands of times I have asked the Lord for the means to build these two homes and now I have to the full received the answer."[8]

Consider what Müller was saying. At one point in his life, he testified that he received thirty thousand definite answers to prayer *on the day of asking*. But when it came to the really large requests, he believed that the bigger the need, the greater the number of prayers required in order to secure it. If one request does not obtain the answer, have the faith to offer two. If two is insufficient, try four. If four is inadequate, show your trust in God by asking eight times. Possibly the request is such that it will require thousands of petitions before the answer is given.

D. L. Moody appreciated the ministry of Müller in the arena of persistent petitioning. He wrote, "Some people think God does not like to be troubled with our constant coming and asking. The only way to trouble God is not to come at all. He encourages us to come to Him repeatedly and press our claims."[9]

What large answers do you seek? Continual coming to him for supply does not bother God. Consider the widow of Luke 18:1–8 who received her answer *because of* her continual coming. The present tense of the verb in Matthew 7:7 encourages us to "*keep on* asking" if we hope to receive. God may want you to *keep on* asking as an exercise in faith, offering prayer after prayer, before the answer comes.

Applying Persevering Petitions

What have you been praying about and the Lord has been slow to respond? Instead of asking for it once a day, try sincerely coming to the Lord about it three times a day until he either removes the burden or supplies the need.

Prayer Retreats–Jesus

High-impact leadership can feel like a curse after a while. The more success we have, the more responsibilities we are given, the higher the expectations we face, and the tougher the criticisms we endure. The more effective we become, the more we are in demand, and the busier our schedule becomes. Often the pace and pressure are so intense we get drained and dry. Many leaders have fallen apart, the victims of their own success . . . but not Jesus.

After Jesus launched his itinerant ministry, his fame grew. The crowds multiplied, the pace increased, the stakes were amplified, and the energy expended intensified. So how did Jesus deal with the pressures of high-impact ministry? Luke tells us. "But Jesus often withdrew to lonely places and prayed" (Luke 5:16).

Human nature, when pressed by increased demands and blessed by greater opportunities, is always tempted to spend less time alone in prayer. Yet Jesus shows us that for the high-impact spiritual leader, the greater the pressure to reduce our time in prayer, the greater the need to maintain and even increase it.

Frequent seasons, lonely places, and quiet times in prayer were Jesus' secret for keeping his spiritual batteries charged and his emotional tanks full. Overbusy lives, packed schedules, hurried, hustling, bustling lifestyles are contrary to the leadership life of Jesus. The Luke 5:16 citing is not an isolated incident. Jesus *often* withdrew to lonely places and prayed (see Matthew 4:1–11; 14:13, 23; 17:1–9; 26:36–46; Mark 1:35; 6:31; Luke 6:12).

If Jesus felt the need to flee to prayer to relieve pressure, how much more should you and I? If he took personal prayer retreats, maybe we should do so as well.

How to Take a Personal Prayer Retreat

Personal prayer retreats have been a great joy and aid to my prayer life. They have helped me briefly escape the pressures of leadership and untangle gnarled ministry issues. Some of my prayer retreats have extended over several nights, while others last just an afternoon. Lately, I most often do them when I'm driving alone for several hours headed to a speaking engagement.

The benefits of such a personal prayer retreat are manifold. Stress is reduced and life is placed back into perspective. Spiritual tanks are refueled. Soul space is created for greater capacity to sense God and hear his voice, both during the retreat and in the coming days. I feel like my anointing to minister is recharged and enhanced. Most of all, I sense that I will be much better prepared to face whatever challenges arise in the coming days.

Let me give you some suggestions for how you can take a personal prayer retreat:

1. Get away from the routine. I have been privileged to take several personal prayer retreats, and I assure you I have never regretted any of them. When money was tight, I would stay at my parents' house while they were out of town. Other times I have stayed at a lodge or cabin in the woods, a Catholic retreat house in the city, a college dorm room in the summer, or a hotel room. The prayer retreat may be as short as a few hours, or several days. The point is to get away from people for a time so you can give your entire attention to God.

2. Start with some solitude and rest. Depending on the amount of time I have, I might spend the first period in absolute solitude and silence while I fast. If I have been very busy and am worn down, I might start with a nap. It is amazing how much better you can pray when you have had some rest.

3. Create some space in your soul. During the first section of my prayer retreat I try to be still and know that he is God. I might read a large chunk of Scripture, such as Isaiah, chapters 40–66, or maybe I'll slowly read a section of a very challenging biography or other book. Generally, I take a few walks out in the beauty of nature. Mostly, I'm simply trying to clear some space in my cluttered soul.

4. Enter his gates with thanksgiving and his courts with praise. I frequently use my journal to pray. I often begin with a season of adoration and praise, listing all the awesome attributes or maybe the mighty names of God. Then I move to thanksgiving. I may list a hundred items for which I'm grateful including material and physical blessings, people, events, opportunities, trials, and answers to prayer.

5. Confess sin. I ask the Holy Spirit to show me every unresolved sin in my life. He usually does not hesitate to bring one item after another to my mind that I neglected to confess in the busyness of the previous weeks. Then I usually get up and walk around a bit.

When I sit back down, he will often slice deeper, showing me buried heart sins and attitudes that have accumulated through the previous months. As I ask for and receive forgiveness, the measure of joy that explodes in my soul may be very intense. I feel profoundly clean and closer to the Father than I have in weeks.

6. Make your requests known to God. The last, and usually longest, section of my prayer time is spent in supplication. This may take different tacks. I might list and pray for dozens of people. Or possibly the focus is on upcoming situations, leadership challenges, or ministry opportunities. It may center on passionately praying back to the Father some of the Bible promises that seem relevant to my current chapter in life.

Frequently my prayer time turns back to several of the big requests I have felt led to pray for through the past few years. I may thank God for the progress being made, but always I'm doggedly persistent to keep on asking, seeking, and knocking until the answer fully comes. For me, this season of intensely personal pouring my heart out to God frequently turns into song, where the requests flow into rhyme. (If you have ever heard me sing, you would understand one reason why I only do this when I'm alone).

7. Reflect on and record what God might have been saying to you. I often conclude by trying to write down the main items God was seemingly saying to me during our time away together. This could be one sentence, a verse, or a lengthy list of things to remember in the coming weeks.

Instant Message, or Arrow, Prayers—Nehemiah

There are occasions when you don't have time for a sweet hour of prayer, or a nifty fifty, or even a five-minute prayer. There is no time or opportunity to go aside and pray. You are in the middle of something and you need help and you need it *now*. All you can do is silently shoot a one-line, or even one-word, "arrow prayer" toward heaven. You could also call it an "instant message prayer." It works. Ask Nehemiah.

In 445 BC, Jerusalem was held by the Persians. The once proud city lay in ruin and reproach because the protective wall that surrounded it was still broken down. In the ancient world, a city without walls was desperately and dangerously vulnerable to thieving marauders and military invaders. Nehemiah, the cupbearer of King Artaxerxes I of Persia, was brokenhearted for the condition of Jerusalem and was burdened to do something about it. So he planned to approach Artaxerxes and ask for permission to return to Jerusalem to rebuild the wall.

This was a highly risky venture. If the temperamental king did not like this petition, he might very easily have Nehemiah killed. But Nehemiah knew he had to ask. Look at what happened:

> In the month of Nisan in the twentieth year of King Artaxerxes, when wine was brought for him, I took the wine and gave it to the king. I had not been sad in his presence before; so the king

asked me, "Why does your face look so sad when you are not ill? This can be nothing but sadness of heart."

I was very much afraid, but I said to the king, "May the king live forever! Why should my face not look sad when the city where my fathers are buried lies in ruins, and its gates have been destroyed by fire?"

The king said to me, "What is it you want?"

Then I prayed to the God of heaven, and I answered the king, "If it pleases the king and if your servant has found favor in his sight, let him send me to the city in Judah where my fathers are buried so that I can rebuild it." (Nehemiah 2:1–5, emphasis added).

"Then I prayed to the God of heaven." Nehemiah was in the fearful presence of a powerful king. He was understandably afraid, and yet, the king had asked a question that opened the door for Nehemiah to offer his request. Nehemiah's fate hung in the balance, as did that of the Jews. So quickly, silently, Nehemiah "prayed to the God of heaven." We don't know exactly what he prayed— maybe "Help," or "Remember me," or "Give me success," or "Guide my words," or "Don't let me mess this up." But we know that he prayed an arrow prayer . . . and God answered.

Then the king, with the queen sitting beside him, asked me, "How long will your journey take, and when will you get back?" It pleased the king to send me; so I set a time.

I also said to him, "If it pleases the king, may I have letters to the governors of Trans-Euphrates, so that they will provide me safe-conduct until I arrive in Judah? And may I have a letter to Asaph, keeper of the king's forest, so he will give me timber to make beams for the gates of the citadel by the temple and for the city wall and for the residence I will occupy?" And because the gracious hand of my God was upon me, *the king granted my requests.* (Nehemiah 2:6–8, emphasis added).

Arrow prayers are short, direct sentences directed like arrows toward the heart of God. In the quotation from Spurgeon given earlier in this chapter he called them "sparks," "hand grenades," and "darts." They can be petitions ("Help me," "Forgive me," "Use me," "Remember me," "Give me wisdom," "Give me strength," "Be with me"). Arrow prayers might be intercessions ("Lord, have mercy on them," "Protect them," "God bless them"). They could be words of praise and thanks ("Thank you, Lord," "You are awesome, O God," "We worship you, O Lord"). The effectiveness of concise, simple, arrow payers is that there have been previous extended times of truly touching the heart of God in prayer.

Praying the Scriptures—Martin Luther

When asked by his barber and good friend, Peter Beskendorf, for some practical guidance on how to prepare oneself for prayer, Luther responded by writing a brief book, *A Simple Way to Pray, for a Good Friend.* It was first published in the spring of 1535. After nearly five hundred years, his instruction continues to offer words of spiritual nurture for us.

Luther counseled using the Lord's Prayer, the Psalms, the Ten Commandments, and the Apostles' Creed as models and guidelines for how to structure our prayers and as a way to connect Christian teaching with our spiritual disciplines. He recommended praying through them phrase by phrase. Luther said, "Nothing can be said here about the part of faith and Holy Scriptures [in prayer] because there would be no end to what could be said. With practice one can take the Ten Commandments on one day, a psalm or chapter of Holy Scripture the next day, and use them as flint and steel to kindle a flame in the heart."[10]

Luther taught that Bible study is like a garland of four twisted strands. Each strand can be posed as a question and an aspect of prayer. The four questions are:

1. What is the teaching/meaning for me?
2. What prayer of thanksgiving does this prompt?
3. What confession or lament does it evoke?
4. What is the prayer petition?

Applying Praying the Scriptures

I challenge you to take the passages Luther suggested or another section, such as the Beatitudes or the Twenty-Third Psalm. Read it carefully and turn each phrase into a prayer or prayers as you weave a garland of prayer.

Frank Familiarity—Billy Sunday and Moses

"He talks to Jesus as familiarly as he talks with his associates," was the way an observer described the prayers of Billy Sunday.[11] From famous baseball player to mighty evangelist, William Ashley "Billy" Sunday (1862–1935) is still remembered for his energetic preaching style and large, successful evangelistic campaigns across the United States. In his lifetime, Billy Sunday addressed more than one hundred million people without the aid of loudspeakers, TV, or radio.

A former National League outfielder, Sunday was converted to Christ in the 1880s and became the most celebrated and influential American evangelist during the first two decades of the twentieth century. As many as a million people came forward at his invitations, and he may have personally preached the gospel of Jesus Christ to more people than any other person in history up to that time. He was a bold, passionate, vibrant, robust, energetic preacher who captivated his audiences. A strong supporter of Prohibition, he played a significant role in the adoption of the Eighteenth Amendment.

Counter to the stuffy formality of the religious establishment of his day, Sunday offered disarmingly direct, childlike petitions to the Lord both in the privacy of his room *and* from the platform of his crusades. As a former baseball player, his prayers were peppered with colloquial figures of speech. Read the unconventionally bold frankness in these recorded prayers:

> O God, help this old world. May the men who have been drunkards be made better; may the men who beat their wives and curse their children come to Jesus; may the children who have feared to hear the footsteps of their father rejoice again when they see the parent coming up the steps to their homes. Bring the church up to help the work.[12]

> O Lord, there are a lot of people who step up to the collection plate and fan [strike out].[13]

> Some of them are dying on second and third base, Lord, and we don't want that.[14]

Frank Familiarity, 1450 BC

Billy Sunday certainly wasn't the first to speak to the Lord with direct familiarity. Several millennia prior, the great spiritual giant Moses erected a tent where he would go each day to meet with the Lord. God's presence there was so thick and obvious, it was visible as a cloud coming down and hovering at the entrance when Moses went in. Moses called that place the Tent of Meeting. I would love to have been a fly on the wall and to have seen and heard what occurred there. The Scripture gives the briefest glimpse into the tent. Stunningly it reveals a frank and familiar conversation between God and man. "The LORD would speak to Moses face to face, as a man speaks with his friend" (Exodus 33:11).

Applying Frank Familiarity

In its purest sense, prayer is simply talking with God. Practice praying out loud. Consciously talk with the Lord as speaking with a friend (which is just what you'll be doing).

Group Prayer Meetings—Henrietta Mears

We have already discussed the incredibly effective "Teacher," Henrietta Mears. As educational director at Hollywood (California) Presbyterian Church, her college-and-career Sunday school class and midweek Bible study meetings were legendary. The crowds were large and enthusiastic, people were saved, and lives were changed. What can we learn from her success?

On Sunday mornings, her huge college department always had a half-hour prayer session with her before each meeting.[15] On Wednesday nights, the leaders met with her an hour beforehand to get down on their knees, confess their weaknesses, and implore the Holy Spirit to empower them. They prayed that the visitors might accept Christ. They prayed for a moving of God's presence. One of her biographers observed, "Teacher was always there, and the greatest effectiveness of her ministry was generated in these and similar prayer times."[16]

Listening and Smuggling Prayer—"Brother Andrew"

Andy van der Bijl (1928–) was one of six children born to a poor, deaf blacksmith in the Netherlands. With little training, he was deeply passionate about being used by God as a missionary. You may know him as "Brother Andrew," famous for his exploits smuggling Bibles into Communist countries during the cold war.

In missionary training school he learned the value of "quiet time" and made it his daily practice to spend time with the Lord every morning in Bible reading and prayer. He had been praying diligently about getting a visa to enter Yugoslavia but had been completely unsuccessful. His biographer writes, "One morning he heard a voice say, 'Today you will get a visa for Yugoslavia.'"[17] By the end of the day, he not only had the "impossible to get" visa to enter Yugoslavia, but also a nice new car to drive.

After driving across Europe to Yugoslavia, Andy arrived at the forbidding border. There he prayed what he came to call the "Smuggler's Prayer": "Lord, in my luggage I have Scriptures that I want to take to Your children across this border. When You were on earth You made blind eyes see. Now, I pray, make seeing eyes blind. Do not let the guards see those things You do not want them to see."[18]

Amazingly, as the guards went through his luggage they did not notice the religious literature scattered through his folded shirts and clothes. After that, the smuggling scene answer to prayer was repeated over and over again as "God's Smuggler" snuck Bibles into Hungary, East Germany, Romania, Bulgaria, Russia, and China, as well as Turkey and Saudi Arabia.

Prayer-Walking—Abraham and Joshua

When God gave Abraham the pledge of the Promised Land, he also gave Abraham an intriguing command to "Go, walk through the length and breadth of the land, for I am giving it to you" (Genesis 13:17). Steps of faith would ultimately be the key to securing the land.

When Joshua took the reins from Moses, he had the big job of leading the people into the Promised Land and conquering it. Knowing how fearful Joshua was of such a huge undertaking, the Lord gave him many wonderful promises. One had originally been given to Moses: "Every place where you set your foot will be yours" (Deuteronomy 11:24; also see Joshua 1:3).

Joshua began to experience the power of this promise when he led the people to follow the priests as they stepped into the flooded

Jordan River by faith *before* it opened for them to cross. When the priests stepped in by faith, the waters parted and they and the other Israelites passed on dry land (Joshua 3:15–17).

Next, Joshua had an encounter with the Commander-in-Chief of the Lord's army, Jesus Christ. Jesus commanded him to "Take off your sandals, for the place where you are standing is holy" (Joshua 5:15).

After that, Joshua saw the promise kept again in a different way when he faced the task of conquering Jericho. Located near the Jordan, Jericho was the key to conquering the Promised Land. As the city of moon worship, God wanted it destroyed.

But that posed a problem.

The walls around this impregnable city were so thick they said you could drive a chariot around the top. There was no army on earth that could hope to attack Jericho and succeed. Therefore, the Lord gave Joshua a unique battle plan.

He was to take the ark of the covenant and march his army behind it around the city once a day for six days as the priests blew their trumpets. On the seventh day, they were to march around it seven times. On the last time around, the people were to shout for victory.

When they shouted the victory call, the walls fell in. Jericho was breached and then totally destroyed (Joshua 6:20, 21). Again the faith to step out in obedience to the Lord was rewarded.

Since the days of Joshua, Christian leaders have led their people to take steps of faith. Through the years it has not been uncommon for pastors to lead their people to literally walk around a piece of property claiming it for the Lord as the site of their new church facilities. Others have prayed in every seat of their church's sanctuary asking God to fill those seats and touch everyone who will be seated in them on Sunday.

In recent days some have adapted the principles applied by Joshua as a means of evangelism and spiritual warfare. They call it prayer-walking. Prayer-walking has been defined as "praying on-site with insight." Done corporately or as individuals, prayer-walking is a form of intercession that takes the intercessor to the battle.

Breaking Demonic Oppression

Several years ago, John Dawson, now international president of Youth with a Mission, moved into a gang-infested neighborhood in inner-city Los Angeles. He mobilized his team to use prayer-walking as a means of ministry:

> Several years ago my staff and I went on a prayer walk around our neighborhood. We stood in front of every house, rebuked Satan's work in Jesus' name and prayed a revelation of Jesus in the life of each family. We are still praying. There is still a long way to go, but economic and spiritual transformation is evident. There are times when demonic oppression almost crushed my soul. I received a death threat. My tires were slashed. I was often depressed at the sight of boarded-up houses, unemployed youth, and disgruntled families, but I was determined to not run away.
>
> Today there are at least nine Christian families in the block where I live, and there is a definite sense of the Lord's peace. The neighborhood is no longer disintegrating. People are renovating their houses and a sense of community is being established around the Christian families.[19]

Impacting a City

When I was a pastor, we saw a definite change in the spiritual climate of our city when we began to institute several forms of "prayer walks." First, I began to drive the perimeter of the city several nights a week, claiming it for God. I would drive by churches and pray for the pastors, then drive by the schools and pray for the teachers and children.

Second, I organized the evangelical pastors in our town to pray in each other's churches once a month. When we started there were only three of us. But within a few years, God had moved the theologically liberal, spiritually cold pastors out of the churches in town, one by one. Incredibly, twelve pastors were faithfully meeting each month to pray for revival in our town. A few years later these pastors worked together to deliver a video of the *Jesus* film to every home in our town. We got the gospel to eight thousand homes, encompassing more than thirty thousand people, in one day! Barna Research did follow-up on our venture and discovered that more than 600 people had trusted Christ as a direct result.

Third, I loaded up our church bus once a month to pray in the parking lot of every church, school, and bar in town. When we started our late-night prayer drives, our schools were in terrible shape. The new superintendent, among other things, had been aggressively hiring lesbians to fill every open principal and teacher position he could. One Halloween, a group of about forty of us got off our church bus, held hands, and began praying at the school board building. We fervently prayed that God would change the superintendent one way or another. We prayed that God would give us a godly superintendent.

We did not know it, but at that exact time the school board was meeting to discuss all the problems with the new superintendent. The next day I discovered that at the very time we were praying outside the building, inside the building the school board members were voting to fire the superintendent. A few months later they replaced him with a godly Christian man who served as an elder in his church!

Impacting a Neighborhood

Sally, one of our small-group leaders, prayer-walked her neighborhood every day, interceding for the salvation of each family. She also served her neighbors and took an interest in their children. As a result she spiritually impacted her neighbors.

One day she asked if she could use one of the large classrooms at the church after the next week's worship service. When asked why, she replied, "Nearly a dozen of my neighbors and their children are being baptized here next week. We want to throw a party in honor of their baptism."

Advice

1. Keep a low profile. Prayer-walking is usually not aimed at attracting attention. Friends or family stroll two by two through their own neighborhoods, schools, or workplaces, praying as they go. The idea is "being on the scene without making one."

2. Pray God's promises with specific homes, schools, churches, or work sites in view.

3. Strive to see people, neighborhoods, churches, and schools as God might view them.

4. Realize that your ministry may be like John the Baptist's, preparing the way for future ministry. Your prayers may be what are needed to soften hearts and ready them for the gospel.

APPLICATION WORKSHEET

What are two or three key thoughts you want to remember from this chapter?

1.

2.

3.

Which of these best practices is something you need to put into your prayer life?

How do you plan on applying it?

CHAPTER 10

Putting It All Together

As I STUDIED these nine secrets of a highly effective prayer life, I was more challenged than I expected. Reading the stories and considering the quotations of this vast variety of leaders has motivated me to ramp up my prayer life. Now the questions are:

1. What are the big things God wanted me to learn?
2. What are the main areas God wants me to focus on now?
3. What am I going to do about it?
4. What specific steps of application will I follow through on?

Inspiration and information without application leads to frustration. This may be the most important chapter in this book because it helps you apply to your life what you have learned.

Prayer Life Lessons

Look back through the application section at the end of each chapter. Read what you recorded under the question: "What are two or three key thoughts you want to remember from this chapter?" Now list the two or three biggest ones you got from reading this book.

1.

2.

3.

Prayer Life Inventory

Respond to each statement as honestly as possible.

Chapter 1

1. I firmly believe that prayer makes a difference in me and in the world around me.   Yes ☐ No ☐
2. I have seen God answer my prayers in the past and believe he wants to do much more in the future.   Yes ☐ No ☐

Chapter 2

3. I spend a sufficient amount of time in prayer each day.   Yes ☐ No ☐
4. That amount of time usually is _____ minutes a day.   Yes ☐ No ☐
5. I have and maintain a consistent daily prayer time.   Yes ☐ No ☐
6. My prayer time is the right length of time right now.   Yes ☐ No ☐
7. I have and maintain several daily prayer times.   Yes ☐ No ☐
8. My prayer times are the right lengths of time right now.   Yes ☐ No ☐
9. I have a good place(s) where I regularly pray.   Yes ☐ No ☐

Chapter 3

10. I spend a sufficient amount of time praying   Yes ☐ No ☐
    for others each day.
11. When I pray for others, I do more than merely   Yes ☐ No ☐
    go through the motions. I'm often moved to
    the point of tears.

Chapter 4

12. I have recruited several people to pray for   Yes ☐ No ☐
    me regularly.
13. I regularly keep those people aware of my   Yes ☐ No ☐
    prayer needs.
14. I also have at least one person I pray with   Yes ☐ No ☐
    several days a week.

Chapter 5

15. I go to the Lord with all my daily needs.   Yes ☐ No ☐
16. I consistently turn my worries into prayers.   Yes ☐ No ☐

Chapter 6

17. In the past, I have fasted from food for   Yes ☐ No ☐
    spiritual reasons for at least a twenty-four-
    hour period.
18. I fast for spiritual reasons on a regular basis.   Yes ☐ No ☐
19. In the past, I have completed an extended   Yes ☐ No ☐
    fast of at least three days.

Chapter 7

20. My prayers are characterized by faith   Yes ☐ No ☐
    and boldness.
21. I pray God's promises back to him.   Yes ☐ No ☐

22. I boldly bring very specific prayer requests   Yes ☐ No ☐
    to God.
23. I honor the Lord by asking him for big things   Yes ☐ No ☐
    only he can do.

Chapter 8

24. I have a good plan for prayer that, in some   Yes ☐ No ☐
    fashion, incorporates the elements of adoration,
    confession, thanksgiving, and supplication
    (ACTS).
25. I consistently speak words of praise to   Yes ☐ No ☐
    the Lord.
26. I confess my sins on a very regular basis.   Yes ☐ No ☐
27. I consistently give thanks to the Lord for he   Yes ☐ No ☐
    is good and his love endures forever.
28. I keep a list of the things I'm praying for.   Yes ☐ No ☐

Chapter 9

29. Beyond my set prayer times, I find myself   Yes ☐ No ☐
    praying all throughout the day.
30. When I believe God wants to answer a   Yes ☐ No ☐
    request, I will continue to pray for it over
    and over, day after day, until he provides.
31. I regularly shoot arrow prayers to the Lord.   Yes ☐ No ☐
32. I regularly pray the Scriptures.   Yes ☐ No ☐
33. I regularly take some type of prayer retreats.   Yes ☐ No ☐
34. I could be described as speaking to the   Yes ☐ No ☐
    Lord with frank familiarity as one talks
    with a friend.
35. I meet with my leaders for prayer at least   Yes ☐ No ☐
    once a week.
36. I have made some type of prayer-walking a   Yes ☐ No ☐
    part of my prayer ministry.

Prayer Life Assessment

Read back over your responses to the Prayer Life Inventory. Circle all the ones in which your answer was negative. For example, as I worked through the inventory I was not happy with my responses to questions 18 and 23. I realized I needed to fast and pray more faithfully. If the early church could do it two days a week, I could do it at least one day a week. I also determined to do a three-day fast several times in the next couple of months, combining that with boldly asking the Lord for a handful of big things.

As you prayerfully consider each negative response, pick a few areas where you are confident the Lord wants you to make changes. Write those areas needing change below.

1.

2.

3.

4.

5.

Prayer Life Application

Looking back over the areas you need to change, prayerfully brainstorm the specific applications you can make. For example, as I took the inventory, I realized I had also gotten away from having a prayer partner (question 14). So my step of application was to begin to pray with my eldest son, over the phone several nights a week. I have done it the last few weeks and it has been noticeably good for both of us.

Write the steps of application you plan to take for each area:

1.

2.

3.

4.

5.

Prayer Life Goal

I have always felt like a book was worth reading if it either gave me one big idea, a great quotation, or a life lesson I could remember the rest of my life, *or* if it gave one exceptionally good idea I could apply to my daily life. Hopefully this book did both for you. If you had to summarize in one sentence that big idea, great quotation, or life lesson, or that one outstanding idea you got out of reading this book, what would it be? Write it below:

Ask God to help you remember and apply it. Ask him to change your life and leadership through it.

Spiritual Leaders Studied

ONLY GOD can judge the true greatness of a leader. For this work, I tried to study many of the best-known names in the Bible and church history. Of those chosen, all had a marked spiritual impact. They cover a variety of leadership posts from missions to the pastorate, to education, to parachurch ministries. They span the entire spectrum of theological thought among evangelicals.

The quotes and anecdotes came from leaders of whom I could find evidence of accurate information regarding their prayer lives. Some of the ones listed led extremely large works, while others led smaller ministries. Yet, all made a spiritual difference.

Realize that my list is certainly far from exhaustive. I'm keenly aware that there are many great leaders from other countries and cultures, yet I was unable to access much information about their prayer lives as I wrote this book. So, while I acknowledge there are many other great spiritual leaders we *could* have studied for this book, I'm content that the cross section was broad enough to give us prayer insights and disciplines we all can use to become more effective spiritual leaders. Below I have listed those leaders in alphabetical order.

Bible

1. Abraham
2. Asa
3. Daniel
4. David
5. Elijah
6. Gideon
7. Hezekiah
8. Jehoshaphat
9. Jesus
10. John
11. Moses
12. Nehemiah
13. Paul
14. Peter
15. Samuel
16. Solomon

Other

17. Augustine
18. Henry Blackaby
19. Richard Blackaby
20. William Booth
21. E. M. Bounds
22. Bill Bright
23. John Bunyan
24. John Calvin
25. Amy Carmichael
26. Paul Y. Cho
27. John Chrysostom
28. John Dawson
29. Wesley Duewel
30. Dick Eastman

31. Jonathan Edwards
32. LeRoy Eims
33. Jim Elliot
34. Jerry Falwell
35. Charles Finney
36. Ronnie Floyd
37. George Fox
38. Billy Graham
39. Jack Hayford
40. Jan Hus
41. Bill Hybels
42. John Hyde
43. David Jeremiah
44. Adoniram Judson
45. John Knox
46. C. S. Lewis
47. H. B. London
48. Max Lucado
49. Martin Luther
50. John Maxwell
51. Joe McKeever
52. Henrietta Mears
53. D. L. Moody
54. George Müller
55. Andrew Murray
56. Bob Pierce
57. Leonard Ravenhill
58. John R. Rice
59. J. O. Sanders
60. Edith Schaeffer
61. Francis Schaeffer
62. Chuck Smith
63. Charles H. Spurgeon
64. Billy Sunday

65. Charles Swindoll
66. Hudson Taylor
67. Corrie ten Boom
68. Tertullian
69. R. A. Torrey
70. Elmer Towns
71. A. W. Tozer
72. Dawson Trotman
73. Andy van der Bijl, or "Brother Andrew"
74. Charles Wesley
75. John Wesley
76. Susanna Wesley
77. Warren Wiersbe

Notes

Introduction

1. J. O. Sanders, *Spiritual Leadership* (Chicago: Moody, 1974), 82.

2. Ibid.

3. Ibid., 84.

4. Henry and Richard Blackaby, *Spiritual Leadership* (Nashville: B&H Publishing Group, 2001), 151.

5. Peter Wagner, as quoted in George Barna, ed., *Leaders on Leadership* (Ventura, CA: Regal Books, 1997), 282, 295.

6. Charles Swindoll, *Hand Me Another Brick* (Nashville: Thomas Nelson, 1978), 37.

7. Wesley Duewel, *Ablaze For God* (Grand Rapids, MI: Zondervan, 1989), 217.

8. Ibid., 214.

9. Andrew Murray, *With Christ in the School of Prayer* (Grand Rapids, MI: Zondervan, 1983), xii.

10. J. C. Ryle, *A Call to Prayer* (Grand Rapids, MI: Baker Book House, 1976), 14–15.

11. Quoted in Duewel, 211.

12. E. M. Bounds, *Prayer and Praying Men* (Grand Rapids, MI: Baker, 1997), 13, 24.

13. Sanders, 84.

14. For a complete listing of leaders studied, please see the appendix.

Chapter One

1. William Brehm, *Why Should We Pray?* Be Ready! http://www .beready.org/whypray.html.

2. "Statistics About Pastors," Maranathalife.com, http://www .maranathalife.com/lifeline/stats.htm.

3. "Study shows only 16% of Protestant ministers are very satisfied with their personal prayer lives," Ellison Research, http://www.ellisonresearch .com/ERPS%20II/release_16_prayer.htm.

4. Win Arn, *The Pastor's Manual for Effective Ministry* (Monrovia, CA: Church Growth, 1988), 41.

5. Andrew Murray, *The Prayer Life* (Springdale, PA: Whitaker House, 1981), 8.

6. Joel Comiskey, *Home Group Cell Explosion* (Houston: Touch Publications, 1998), 34.

7. Blackabys, 151.

8. Charles Spurgeon, *Twelve Sermons on Prayer* (Grand Rapids, MI: Baker Book House, 1971), 31.

9. R. A. Torrey, *The Power of Prayer* (Grand Rapids, MI: Zondervan, 1924), 17.

10. Hudson Taylor, as quoted in Sanders, 82.

11. Leonard Ravenhill, *Why Revival Tarries* (Minneapolis: Bethany House, 1979), 153.

12. John Chrysostom, as quoted in Ravenhill, 153.

13. Martin Luther, as quoted in Sanders, 76.

14. S. D. Gordon, *Quiet Talks on Prayer* (Grand Rapids, MI: Baker Book House, reprinted 1980), 15.

15. Wesley Duewel, *Touch the World through Prayer* (Grand Rapids, MI: Zondervan, 1986), 11.

16. John Wesley and John Calvin, quoted by Peter Wagner in *Prayer Shield* (Ventura, CA: Regal Books, 1992), 29.

17. Billy Graham quoted by Cort Flint, ed., *The Quotable Billy Graham* (Anderson, SC: Droke House, 1966), 154.

18. Richard Foster, *Prayer: Finding the Heart's True Home* (San Francisco: HarperSanFrancisco, 1992), xxx.

19. LeRoy Eims, *Be the Leader You Were Meant to Be* (Carol Stream, IL: Victor Books, 1975), 19.

20. Jack Hayford, *Prayer Is Invading the Impossible* (Orlando, FL: Bridge-Logos Publishers, 2002), xxx.

21. E. M. Bounds, *The Weapon of Prayer* (Grand Rapids, MI: Baker Book House, 1931), xxx.

22. David Jeremiah, *Prayer: The Great Adventure* (Sisters, OR: Multnomah Publishers, 1997), 40–41.

23. Billy Graham, as quoted in Flint, 153.

24. Gordon, 31–38.

25. Chuck Smith, *Effective Prayer Life*, Calvary Chapel, http://www3 .calvarychapel.com/library/smith-chuck/books/epl.htm.

26. Dick Eastman, *Love on Its Knees* (Tarrytown, NY: Fleming Revell, 1989), 65.

27. Duewel, *Touch the World*, 206.

28. Joe McKeever, "What Pastors Need #3: A Good Prayer Life," Joe McKeever.com, August 31, 2004, http://www.joemckeever.com/mt/ archives/000065.html.

29. Wagner, 64.

30. "Statistics about Pastors," Maranathalife.com, http://www .maranathalife.com/lifeline/stats.htm.

31. Kevin Miller, "10 Telling Statistics about Pastors: Research on money, sex, and power," July 12, 2000, christianitytoday.com, http://www .christianitytoday.com/leaders/newsletter/cln00712.html.

32. Duewel, *Touch the World*, 216.

Chapter Two

1. Gordon, 211.

2. Ibid., 209.

3. E. M. Bounds, *The Reality of Prayer* (Grand Rapids, MI: Baker Book House, 1978), 69, 73.

4. Martin Luther, as quoted in E. M. Bounds, *Power through Prayer* (Grand Rapids, MI: Zondervan, 1962), 37, emphasis added.

5. Howard and Geraldine Taylor, *Hudson Taylor's Spiritual Secret*, (Chicago: Moody Press, 1932), 235.

6. Ibid., 236.

7. Betty Lee Skinner, *Daws: The Story of Dawson Trotman, Founder of the Navigators* (Grand Rapids, MI: Zondervan, 1974), 53.

8. Bounds, *Power through Prayer*, 42.

9. Peter Wagner, *Churches That Pray* (Ventura, CA: Regal Books, 1993), 25.

10. Paul Y. Cho, *Prayer: Key to Revival* (Waco, TX: Word Books, 1984), 18.

11. Bill Hybels, *Too Busy Not to Pray* (Downers Grove, IL: InterVarsity Press, 1988), 9.

12. Ibid., 10.

13. Cho, xxx.

14. Basil Miller, *George Müller: Man of Faith and Miracles* (Minneapolis: Bethany Fellowship, 1941), 49.

15. Charles Spurgeon, "Pray Without Ceasing," Metropolitan Tabernacle Pulpit, A Sermon Delivered on Lord's Day Morning, March 10, 1872, http://www.spurgeon.org/sermons/1039.htm.

16. John Bunyan, *Christian History Institute Presents Glimpses #202: John Bunyan: A Mender of Pilgrim Souls* © 2007, http://chi.gospelcom.net/GLIMPSEF/Glimpses2/glimpses202.shtml.

17. Martin Luther, *A Simple Way to Pray* (Louisville: Westminster Knox Press, 2000), 193.

18. Jerry Strober and Ruth Tomczak, *Jerry Falwell: Aflame for God* (Nashville, TN: Thomas Nelson, 1979), 25–26.

19. Epiphanius as quoted in Paul Bradshaw, *Daily Prayer in the Early Church* (New York: Oxford University Press, 1982), 9.

20. Tertullian, *De Oratione*, xxiii, xxv, in P.L., I, 1191–93.

21. Hippolytus, *Apostolic Tradition*, as quoted in Boniface Ramsey, *Beginning to Read the Fathers* (Mahwah, NJ: Paulist Press, 1985), 165–66.

22. Adoniram Judson, as quoted in Bounds, *Power through Prayer*, 40.

23. Hybels, 41.

24. Andrew Murray, *With Christ in the School of Prayer* (Grand Rapids, MI: Zondervan, 1983), 11–12.

25. Andrew Murray, *The Prayer Life* (Springdale, PA: Whitaker House, 1981), 97.

26. E. M. Bounds, *Preacher and Prayer* (Grand Rapids, MI: Zondervan, 1982), 36.

Chapter Three

1. Dick Eastman, *No Easy Road* (Grand Rapids, MI: Baker Book House, 1971), 58.

2. Ibid., 57.

3. Wagner, *Prayer Shield*, 26.

4. Wesley Duewel, *Mighty Prevailing Prayer* (Grand Rapids, MI: Zondervan, 1990), 22.

5. Bounds, *Power through Prayer*, 27.

6. Gordon, xxx.

7. Eastman, *Love on Its Knees*, 56.

8. Ibid., 17.

9. Wesley Duewel, *Revival Fires* (Grand Rapids, MI: Zondervan, 1995), 342–45.

10. Francis McGraw, *Praying Hyde* (Minneapolis: Bethany Fellowship, 1970), 16.

11. Kenneth Boa, "The Heart of God," World Vision Resources, http://www.worldvisionresources.com/product_info.php?products_id=289.

12. Duewel, *Ablaze for God*, 243.

13. Story told by H. Begbie in "The Life of General William Booth," as recorded at http://www.jesus-is-savior.com/Great%20Men%20of%20God/general_william_booth.htm.

14. Roger Steer, "Pushing Inward," Christian History and Biography, October 1, 1996 (http://www.ctlibrary.com/ch/1996/Issue52/52h10a.html).

15. D. L. Moody, *Prevailing Prayer* (Chicago: Moody Press, 1987), 100–101.

16. Basil Miller, 146.

17. Ibid.

18. Adapted from Greg Frizzell, *How to Develop a Powerful Prayer Life* (Memphis, TN: Master Design Ministries, 1999), 83.

Chapter Four

1. This true story is adapted from Dave Earley, *Prayer Odyssey* (Shippensburg, PA: Destiny-Image, 2003), 107.

2. Matthew Spinka, *John Hus at the Council of Constance* (New York: Columbia University Press, 1965), 122.

3. H. B. London Jr. and Neil Wiseman, *Pastors at Greater Risk* (Ventura, CA: Regal Books, 2003), 33–60.

4. Bounds, *The Weapon of Prayer*, 125.

5. Bounds, *Power Through Prayer*, 75–76.

6. Wagner, *Prayer Shield*, 9.

7. *Works of Jonathan Edwards*, Volume One, Section III. *Of some particulars that concern all in general*, http://www.ccel.org/ccel/edwards/works1.ix.vi.iii.html.

8. Jonathan Edwards, "The True Excellency of a Gospel Minister," http://www.biblebb.com/files/edwards/theminister.htm.

9. John Maxwell, *Partners in Prayer* (Nashville, TN: Thomas Nelson, 1996), 1.

10. Max Lucado, as quoted in Maxwell, foreword.

11. Charles Spurgeon, as quoted in W. Y. Fullerton, *Charles Haddon Spurgeon* (Chicago: Moody Press, 1966), 262.

12. As quoted in Maxwell, 7.

13. Charles G. Finney, *Memoirs of Revivals of Religion: Published as An Autobiography 1876*, Gospel Truth, http://www.gospeltruth.net/1868Memoirs/memoirsindex.htm.

14. Charles G. Finney, *Principles of Prayer* (Minneapolis: Bethany House, 1980), 74.

15. D. L. Moody, as quoted in William R. Moody, *The Life of Dwight L. Moody* (New York: Fleming H. Revell, 1900), 152.

16. William R. Moody, 153–54.

17. Nancy Pfaff, "Christian Leadership Attributes Dynamic Increase in Effectiveness to the Work of Intercession," *Journal of the American Society for Church Growth,* 1990 edition, 82.

Chapter Five

1. Global Pastors Network, August 2004 newsletter, xxx.

2. Quoted in S. Daniel and M. Rogers, "Burnout and the Pastorate . . . ," *Journal of Psychology and Theology* 9, no. 3 (1981): 232–49.

3. "Coming Out of the Dark: Two Pastors' Journey out of Depression," Wayde I. Goodall and E. Glenn Wagner, *Enrichment Journal,* http:// enrichmentjournal.ag.org/200603/200603_040_journey_pastors.cfm.

4. Quoted by Dustin Benge, "A Dirty Little Secret—Pastoral Depression," August 28, 2007, http://pastorandpeople.wordpress.com/2007/08/ 28/a-dirty-little-secret-%E2%80%93-pastoral-depression/.

5. Gordon, *Quiet Talks on Prayer*, 214.

6. Martin Luther, http://thinkexist.com/quotation/pray-and_let_god/ 160770.html.

7. Basil Miller, 51.

8. George Müller, as quoted in Basil Miller, 47.

9. Ibid., 59.

10. Lyle W. Dorsett, *A Passion for Souls: A Life of D. L. Moody* (Chicago: Moody Press, 1997), 362–64.

11. Billy Graham, *Just As I Am* (New York: HarperCollins, 1997), 148–49.

12. Ibid., 150.

13. Ibid., 155.

14. Ibid., 158.

Chapter Six

1. Epiphanius, as quoted in Duewel, *Mighty Prevailing Prayer*, 180.

2. Augustine, "The Church's Discipline as to Fasting and Abstinence" from *St. Augustine's Prayer Book,* http://www.episcopalnet.org/TRACTS/ fasting.html.

3. *Luther's Little Instruction Book* (The Small Catechism of Martin Luther translated in 1994 for Project Wittenberg by Robert E. Smith), http://www .fullbooks.com/Luthers-Little-Instruction-Book-The-Small.html

4. John Calvin, *Institutes of the Christian Religion*, Book 4, Chapter 12, Section 15, http://www.island-of-freedom.com/caquotes.htm.

5. Arthur Wallis, *God's Chosen Fast*, (Fort Washington, PA: Christian Literature Crusade, 1968), 29–30.

6. Duewel, xxx.

7. Elmer Towns, *Fasting for Spiritual Breakthrough* (Ventura, CA: Regal Books, 1996), 26.

8. Elmer Towns, *Knowing God through Fasting* (Shippensburg, PA: Destiny-Image, 2002), table of contents.

9. Duewel, *Mighty Prevailing Prayer,* 183.

10. Elmer Towns and Douglas Porter, *The Ten Greatest Revivals Ever* (Ann Arbor, MI: Servant Publications, 2000), 63.

11. Duewel, *Revival Fires*, 49–80.

12. Ibid., 92–93.

13. Towns and Porter, 123.

14. Jerry Falwell, quoted in Elmer Towns, *Fasting Can Change Your Life* (Ventura, CA: Regal Books, 1998), 19.

15. Ibid., 19–20.

16. Ibid., 20.

17. Ronnie Floyd, as quoted in Towns, *Fasting Can Change Your Life*, 238.

18. Bill Bright, *The Transforming Power of Fasting and Prayer* (Orlando, FL: New Life Publications, 1997), 18.

19. Bill Bright, "Your Personal Guide to Fasting and Prayer," http:// www.billbright.com/howtofast/.

20. Bill Bright, as quoted in Towns, *Fasting Can Change Your Life*, 104.

Chapter Seven

1. Howard and Geraldine Taylor, 14.

2. Hudson Taylor's sister, as quoted in Howard and Geraldine Taylor, 18.

3. Charles Spurgeon, *God's Checkbook: Daily Drawing on God's Treasury* (Chicago: Moody Press, 1965), ii.

4. Ibid.

5. Quoted in W. Y. Fullerton, 263.

6. Ibid.

7. Ibid.

8. Barbara Hudson Powers, *The Henrietta Mears Story* (Old Tappan, NJ: Fleming H. Revell, 1957), http://www.ccel.us/mears.ch14.html.

9. Duewel, *Touch the World*, 146.

10. Ibid., 147.

11. Charles Finney, *Power from on High* (Ft. Washington, PA: Christian Literature Crusade, 1944), 31.

12. John R. Rice, *Prayer: Asking and Receiving* (Murfreesboro, TN: Sword of the Lord, 1943), 147.

13. Ibid., 154–56.

14. Skinner, 317.

15. Rice, 236.

16. Ibid., 240.

17. Ibid., 249.

18. Ibid.

Chapter Eight

1. C. H. Spurgeon, *The Treasury of David*, Volume V, Psalms 104–18 (Grand Rapids, MI: Baker Book House, 1981), 159.

2. Adolph Saphir in *Lectures on the Lord's Prayer*, as quoted in Spurgeon, 173.

3. Yonggi Cho, as quoted in Elmer Towns, *Praying the Lord's Prayer for Spiritual Breakthrough* (Ventura, CA: Regal Books, 1997), xxx.

4. Sam Wellma, *Corrie ten Boom: Faith amidst Fear* (Uhrichsville, OH: Barbour Publishing, 1995), 152–55.

5. Jerry Falwell, *Falwell: An Autobiography* (Lynchburg, VA: Liberty House Publishers, 1997), 202.

6. Ibid., 210–12.

7. Augustine of Hippo, *Sermons* 336, 1 PL 38, 1472.

8. Duewel, *Touch the World,* 141.

9. *Journal of John Wesley,* "Wesley's Last Hours: By One Who Was Present," http://www.ccel.org/ccel/wesley/journal.vi.xxi.html.

10. John Bunyan, "What Prayer Is," Acadia Online John Bunyan Library, http://acacia.pair.com/Acacia.John.Bunyan/Sermons.Allegories/Discourse.Touching.Prayer/2.html.

11. John R. Rice, *Prayer: Asking and Receiving,* 47.

12. Ibid., 67.

13. Skinner, 89.

14. Ibid., 119.

15. George Müller, *Release the Power of Prayer* (New Kensington, PA: Whitaker House, 1999), back cover.

Chapter Nine

1. Charles Spurgeon, "Pray without Ceasing," http://www.spurgeon.org/sermons/1039.htm.

2. Fullerton, 149.

3. Ibid.

4. Wayland Hoyt, as quoted in Fullerton, 150.

5. George Müller, as quoted in Basil Miller, 59.

6. Ibid., 77.

7. Ibid., 79.

8. Ibid.

9. D. L. Moody, *Prevailing Prayer* (Chicago: Moody Press, 1970), 91–92.

10. Martin Luther, *A Simple Way to Pray* (Louisville: Westminster Knox Press, 2000), 56.

11. William T. Ellis, *"Billy" Sunday: The Man and His Message* (Chicago: Moody Press, 1959), 125.

12. Ibid., 126.

13. Ibid.

14. Ibid., 127.

15. Ethel May Baldwin and David Benson, *Henrietta Mears and How She Did It* (Glendale, CA: Regal Books, 1967), 93.

16. Ibid., 125–26.

17. Alan Millwright, *Brother Andrew: God's Undercover Agent* (Uhrichsville, OH: Barbour Publishing, 1999), 102.

18. Ibid., 106–7.

19. John Dawson, *Taking Our Cities for God* (Lake Mary, FL: Creation House, 1989), 28–29.